THE REFORMATION
OF
OUR WORSHIP

THE REFORMATION
OF
OUR WORSHIP

by

S. F. WINWARD

JOHN KNOX PRESS
RICHMOND, VIRGINIA

British edition published by
THE CAREY KINGSGATE PRESS LIMITED
LONDON, ENGLAND, 1964

American edition published by
JOHN KNOX PRESS,
RICHMOND, VIRGINIA, 1965

CONTENTS

Contents   ix

PREFACE

THIS book is the outcome of an invitation to deliver lectures under the auspices of the Dr W. T. Whitley Lectureship. The chapters (with the exception of chapters I and III) are an expansion of the material delivered as lectures at the South Wales Baptist College Cardiff, in October, and at Regent's Park College, Oxford, in November 1963. I am deeply grateful to the trustees of the Whitley Lectureship for the invitation and opportunity given to me, and to the two college Principals, the Rev. J. Ithel Jones and Dr G. Henton Davies, for the helpful arrangements made, and the warm hospitality afforded me. For a quarter of a century I have worshipped with one particular congregation, and with their consent attempted *some* of the reforms suggested in this book. It is the fruit of past experience and continuing experiment. As such, I hope it may be of some help and encouragement to all those who are endeavouring to reform and enrich the worship of the church, under the guidance of the Word and the Spirit, to the greater glory of God.

Chapter I

WORSHIP, LIFE, AND CULT

1. Worship and life

'Behold, he prayeth; not with the lips alone,
But with the hand and with the cunning brain
Men worship the Eternal Architect.'[1]

THESE words, spoken of the architect of a cathedral, who loved his work and was doing an excellent job, may serve to illustrate a basic truth about worship. True devotion is a specific activity within life, and yet it is also synonymous with the whole of life. The word 'worship' may be used in two different ways, with a limited or an unlimited range of meaning. It may have reference to those specific acts of devotion associated with, although not necessarily confined to, the private room or the sanctuary. It may also be used to describe any attitude or act in which man acknowledges the supreme worth of God. In this latter sense, not only our private prayers and our corporate worship, but the whole of life is involved. This use of the same word with this dual range of meaning, while it often gives rise to confusion of thought, is sound and biblical. We begin with worship as synonymous with life.

Worship is the acknowledgment of the supreme worth of God. The English word derived from the Saxon *weorthscipe* was once more widely used of the ascription of worth to any object, person, or group. There is a fine example of this in the old English of the marriage service of the Book of Common Prayer. As the bridegroom gives the ring to the bride he says, 'with my body I thee worship'. Since, however, no human being has absolute worth, the word has or should have much less than its full meaning when used in such contexts. To acknowledge the worth of another man or woman *as a creature* is indeed pleasing to God, whose will and purpose it is that we should love one another.

[1] D. L. Sayers, *The Zeal of Thy House.*

But to ascribe absolute and unconditional worth to any object, person, or group is idolatry.[1] Using the word with its full meaning and content, worship can only be rightly offered to God himself. 'You shall worship the Lord your God and him only shall you serve.'[2] It is the acknowledgment whether by word or gift, attitude or act, of the *supreme* worth of God; the ascription to the Lord of the glory due to his name. Such an acknowledgment should include and involve the whole of life, character and conduct as well as praises and prayers, work and service as well as offering and sacrifice. It is significant that the New Testament Greek words *latreia* and *leitourgia* are used both of cult and conduct, of worship and service, of liturgy and life. In this connection, it is instructive to set side by side the English translations of the word *latreia* in the Authorised and Revised Standard Versions respectively. 'Present your bodies a living sacrifice, holy, acceptable unto God, which is your reasonable *service* . . . Present your bodies as a living sacrifice, holy and acceptable to God, which is your spiritual *worship*.'[3] Note also how the two versions translate the corresponding verb *latreuein*. 'For there stood by me this night the angel of God, whose I am, and whom I *serve* . . . For this very night there stood by me an angel of the God to whom I belong and whom I *worship*.'[4] Both translations are good, and it cannot be maintained that one is superior to the other, for there is no distinction in the Bible between worship and service. The Hebrew verb, 'to serve' (*abhadh*) when used of God includes every form of service, whether offered in daily life or in ritual acts. In spite of our tragic divorce of worship and service, by calling our assemblies for worship 'services', we still retain something of this biblical insight. The noun *leitourgia* (from which our English word 'liturgy' is derived) and the verb *leitourgein* are also used in the New Testament without any distinction between worship and service. In classical and hellenistic Greek these words were used to describe various services rendered by the citizen to the state. In the New Testament the activity of Zechariah the priest in the temple, the worship offered by the prophets and teachers in the assembly at Antioch, the service rendered by Gentile Christians in contributing money for the needy at Jerusalem, and the ministry of Epaphroditus and the Philippians to Paul in prison, are alike described by these words.[5] No distinction is made between the service of man to

[1] Rom. 1. 25.   [2] Matt. 4. 10.
[3] Rom. 12. 1. A.V. and R.S.V.   [4] Acts 27. 23. A.V. and R.S.V.
[5] Luke 1.23; Acts 13.2; 2 Cor. 9. 12; Phil. 2. 30.

man, and the service of man to God. It is all worship-service, as inseparable as the two sides of a penny. The work of the People of God – liturgy – is one work, whether it is done in the sanctuary or in the world, whether the people are assembled or dispersed. All life, all activity is included. The same truth is patent in the metaphorical use of sacrificial language made by the writers of the New Testament. What are the spiritual sacrifices offered by the Christian priesthood? They include prayers, praises, deeds of kindness, a sharing of possessions with the needy, gifts of money, evangelistic activity, faith, martyrdom, and the consecration of the whole personality.[1] Here also no distinction is made between cult and conduct, worship and service. True worship is synonymous with life, because the true God is the creator of the universe, the ruler of all men and nations, the Lord of all life. As such, he cannot be fenced in or confined to 'the sacred' or 'the religious', or excluded from any sphere of life. 'The great contribution of the Hebrew to religion was that he did away with it.'[2] The opening sentence of William Law's *Serious Call* is an excellent summary of this great biblical insight. 'Devotion is neither private nor public prayer; but prayers, whether private or public, are particular parts or instances of devotion. Devotion signifies a life given, or devoted, to God.'

2. Worship and cult

If true devotion is synonymous with life as a whole, is there then any place or need at all for cult, for a system of religious worship? Has not our Lord Jesus Christ, crucified by priests and scribes, destroyed the cult and abolished religion? 'When the curtain of the temple was torn in two, God judged religion and rejected temples. After this moment temples and churches can only mean places of concentration on the holy which is the ground and meaning of every place.'[3] In fact, cult is present within the new Israel as within the old, for as with the law and the prophets, Jesus Christ has not destroyed but fulfilled it. It has been dethroned and judged, re-created and transformed. Henceforth it is no longer master but servant, no longer an end but a means. As such it may be and should be constantly judged and reformed by the Word and the

[1] 1 Peter 2. 5; Heb. 13. 15, 16; Phil. 4. 18; Rom. 15. 16; Phil. 2. 17; Rom. 12. 1.
[2] J. Macmurray, quoted by G. F. Macleod, *Only One Way Left*, 67.
[3] P. Tillich, *The New Being*, 177–8.

Spirit of God. The presence of cult within the new covenant is necessary for three reasons. The devoted life, whether for the individual or the community, is possible only if there are within it, specific acts of devotion, whether private or public. In this life 'places of concentration on the holy' are necessary, if the whole of life is to be related to God and lived to his glory. For it is only by the consecration of one special part that it is possible to consecrate the whole. If all our days are to be the Lord's, then we must keep holy the Lord's day; if all our meals are to be communion with God, we must celebrate the holy communion. No longer must we say 'this is holy and that is not', but rather 'here we concentrate on the holy in order that every time and every place may be holy'. The sanctification of the common depends upon these specific acts of concentration on the holy. The cult is effective when the worshippers can truly join in the song of the seraphim, 'holy, holy, holy, is the Lord of hosts; *the whole earth* is full of his glory'.[1] Cult is also necessary because man is an animated body. As such, he cannot be satisfied with a general and disembodied piety. Springing from the heart, the devotion of man inevitably seeks outward and visible expression in words and deeds, in personal and communal patterns of action which involve the body, make use of matter, and are perceptible to the senses. Just as the love of a man for his child, wife, or friends, finds overt and concrete expression in words and attitudes, gifts and deeds, so also the abiding sentiments of reverence and love for God will necessarily find expression and embodiment in specific acts of worship. Indeed, the cultic act not only expresses; it may also evoke and strengthen the inner attitude, for love and reverence grow by means of the acts which express them. Furthermore, a man is a social being as well as an animated body and worship is a communal as well as a personal activity. But if men are to worship God *together*, then there must be a customary way of doing things, an accepted pattern of word or deed, whether simple or elaborate. Cult is the customary or agreed expression and embodiment of the worship of a group, and is often regarded in whole or in part as of divine institution and authority. This then is the threefold function of the cult, to transform and consecrate the whole of life, to give outward and concrete expression to the inner devotion and sentiments of the heart, and to enable men to worship God together.

There is uneasy tension and at times open conflict between these two

[1] Isa. 6. 3.

complementary conceptions, the general and the specific, between worship as synonymous with life and cultic acts. The two aspects can be thrown into violent antithesis and regarded as contradictories rather than as complementaries. This tension became acute within Israel in the eighth and seventh centuries B.C. Amos, Hosea, Micah, Isaiah, and Jeremiah denounced the cult and in God's name rejected the cultic acts, the many offerings and costly sacrifices of the people. This prophetic polemic against sacrifices has been taken to mean that the cult *as such* is contrary to God's will and purpose. But this is to ignore other things said by the same prophets, to overlook their own close relationship to the cult, and to interpret literally and unimaginatively hot words spoken in fierce indignation or intense grief. It was against a corrupt cult, the false security it encouraged, the syncretism and depravity associated with it, and the substitution of cultic acts for holy living, that the denunciations of the prophets were directed. They declared that the holy God hates and rejects acts of devotion, however many and costly, which are substitutes for obedience, for humble piety and right personal and social relationships. Only he whose life is devoted to God can offer acceptable acts of devotion. Because God is righteous, cult and conduct must be all of a piece. A one-sided stress on this element in the prophetic message can, however, lead to an error of the opposite kind, no less disastrous in its effects; the assumption that specific acts of devotion are no longer necessary. The great prophetic affirmation, 'to obey is better than sacrifice', can be taken to mean that obedience is possible without sacrifice or any equivalent cultic act. This is the widespread heresy of modern man, who *at his best* substitutes goodness, kindness, and social righteousness for worship, and tacitly assumes that they are all possible without it.

> 'To worship rightly is to love each other,
> Each smile a hymn, each kindly deed a prayer.'[1]

This aspect of truth, presented as if it were the whole truth, encourages men to give up singing hymns, saying prayers, and offering worship. Protestantism has long suffered from a steady propaganda against worship, to which both pulpit and hymnal have contributed. We have tried to encourage holy living by belittling cultic acts. But in the Bible it is everywhere assumed that cultic acts are a part of (not the whole

---

[1] J. G. Whittier, in the hymn, 'O brother man'.

B

of) the service of God. Obedience and love are in fact impossible apart from sacrifice, God's and ours. In the Christian cult, the preaching of the word and the sacrament of the table, the sacrifice made by God in Christ is declared and communicated. At this place of concentration on the holy, we are or can be enabled to offer ourselves both in the sanctuary and in the world as living sacrifices, holy and acceptable to God, which is our reasonable service, our spiritual worship. Cult and conduct, liturgy and life, worship and service belong together. Just because we are concerned with worship as synonymous with the whole of life, we must therefore be concerned with worship as cult.

3. Five selected themes

Because worship includes reverence and piety, obedience and service, a comprehensive treatment of our subject would involve a description of the Christian life as a whole, both communal and personal. We shall confine ourselves in this book to the cult, to the specific acts of worship of the People of God, whether of the old or of the new Israel. Even as thus delimited, worship is still too vast a field, and certain aspects only of it are here selected for study. Five themes have been chosen. This selection, however, is not arbitrary, but is determined by what the author believes to be the basic needs of our protestant worship today. All five aspects alike have to do with the reformation of our contemporary worship. There is widespread dissatisfaction with protestant worship, especially with the worship of the reformed churches and of those which are in part heirs of the puritan tradition. Large numbers of people have expressed this dissatisfaction by staying away from church. They have voted against it 'with their feet'. Among the faithful who have not forsaken the assembling of themselves together, there is a small but growing minority who are deeply troubled and concerned. Beyond the general awareness that many of our church services are irrelevant, unrelated to life, this discontent is largely undefined and inarticulate. What is wrong? How can that which is lacking be supplied? What reforms are required?

(*a*) Christian worship is the human response to the revelation of God in Christ. It is a dialogue, a two-way conversation between God and man, the Spirit-inspired answer to the word declared in the assembly. But in the course of church history, this dialogue has been distorted. The neglect of the preaching of the word before the Reformation led

to an extreme reaction in the opposite direction after it. In some traditions, almost all the stress was placed upon the word, the revelation and
communication of God, and little provision was made for an adequate
response of the congregation in common praise and prayer, in offering
and sacrament. The structure and pattern of our Christian worship
should be so reformed as to reflect and express the dialogue between
God and man as a balanced whole, both in the service of the word and
in the sacraments.

(b) Christian worship should be understood in terms of giving to
God as well as of receiving from God. In many churches this understanding has largely disappeared. In Great Britain today the average
worshipper goes to church to receive rather than to give, to 'get a
blessing' rather than to 'make an offering'.[1] This is to destroy the reciprocal nature of the divine-human encounter, and to pauperize the
recipient of grace. We need to recover the biblical conviction that service is offering, that worship is sacrifice. Such an awareness would go
far to rescue our services from subjectivity and self-centredness. The
ancient call must be re-sounded, 'Ascribe to the Lord the glory due his
name; bring an offering, and come into his courts.'[2]

(c) Christian worship is incarnational and sacramental. Both as revelation and response it should involve the whole personality of man, the
body and the senses as well as thoughts and words, movement and
action as well as listening and understanding. For God is revealed and
communicated through the material and social environment of man,
who is himself flesh. Biblical worship is embodied. Our protestant
worship, however, has been radically intellectualized; it moves too exclusively in the realm of thoughts and words. It is addressed to the ears,
and not to the eyes; it is predominantly notional. All that is directed
to the mind is permitted; all appeal to the senses is suspected or excluded. Reaction against the over-elaborate ceremonial of the Roman
Catholic church has driven us into a mild form of gnosticism. This is
one big reason why our worship makes little appeal to the proletarian,
who does not live and move in the realm of abstract ideas. How then
should our worship be reformed if we take seriously the biblical doctrines of creation and incarnation? What is the true relationship between the inward and the outward in worship?

[1] I owe this contrast to Neville Clark, *Call to Worship*, 12.
[2] Ps. 96. 8.

(*d*) Christian worship is the liturgy, the work of the People of God. This liturgy is the servant of the dialogue, the vehicle of divine revelation and human response. Wherever worship is ordered so as to declare the whole gospel on the one hand, and to ensure the full corporate response of the people on the other, there is liturgy. But in the history of the church, liturgy and liberty, order and freedom, tradition and spontaneity have been thrown into antithesis. In this country, especially since '1662 and all that', Christians tend to think of liturgy in terms of written, inflexible, and enacted services, and of liberty in terms of extempore utterance. There is, however, a growing awareness that this is a false antithesis, together with a demand for both freedom and liturgy. How then should liberty and tradition be combined? Is it possible to have a worship which is both liturgical and free, ordered and charismatic?

(*e*) Christian worship is essentially corporate, communal, congregational. All the members of the Body should be actively involved and engaged in offering worship to God. The most obvious (and some would maintain the greatest) weakness of some forms of protestant worship, is the undue predominance of the one man 'conducting the service'. There is a ministerial monopoly. One man reads, prays, preaches, celebrates: the rest, except in the common praise, listen. How can this state of affairs be rectified? To what extent and in what ways should the laity participate in the worship of the church? What light is shed by the Bible or church history on this problem of congregational participation?

These themes, in this same order, are discussed in the five main chapters of this book.

4. Concerning the method

In our study of these selected subjects, the same method and sequence will be followed in each of the five chapters which follow. First, the theme itself will be stated, and its implications and bearing on our subject indicated. After this preliminary statement, we shall look at our theme in the light of the shining lamp of scripture, turning first to the Old and then to the New Testament. In thus appealing to the Bible, we must be careful to avoid the errors and pitfalls taught us by church history. The scriptures do not provide us with a blue-print for a church service, with a divinely revealed way of doing things. The Bible is not a textbook on the subject of worship. In this connection two errors have been made in the past and continue to be made by some Christians in the present. It is assumed that we must not introduce into our worship anything not explicitly sanctioned in the Bible, and that we must worship today exactly as they did in the Bible, presumably in the apostolic age. Former generations suffered much as a result of the former false assumption. 'The exclusive use of the psalms in praise, the banning of organs and musical instruments, the destruction of all forms of Christian pictorial art, the virtual reduction of worship to a sermon – these became the chief hallmarks of Reformed worship.'[1] The belief that it is wrong to introduce into church worship anything not explicitly commanded in the Bible is still widespread, and the expressions, 'it's not biblical' and, 'it's not in the Bible', are wrongly assumed to be synonymous. Of the latter assumption (that we must worship today exactly as they did in the Bible) no one, of course, imagines that the worship of the new covenant can be simply a continuation without change of the worship of the old covenant. This assumption is often made, however, of the worship of the primitive church. For example, it is usually taken for granted by the Brethren and the Pentecostals that the worship of Christian assemblies today ought to be just like that of the apostolic age. Both these assumptions are a denial of the person and work of the Holy Spirit. There is such a thing as legitimate growth and development, adaptation and change, as well as illegitimate distortion and perversion, accretion and corruption. In our study of cultic words or acts, we are not primarily concerned with what is or is not in the Bible; we are concerned with what is biblical, with that which is in accordance with the revelation of God in Christ contained in the scriptures. It is, of course, by no means easy to distinguish between that which is temporary and accidental, and that which is permanent and essential in the biblical revelation. But this distinction is in fact made by most Christians, including many of those who are unaware of the fact that they do make it. We do not, for example, regard it as *necessary* that we should meet for worship in our homes, wear flowing robes and beards, squat on the floor, speak in Aramaic or Greek, exchange the kiss of peace, or 'speak in a tongue', although these and many other such-like things were customs of the apostles. On the other hand, we are not at liberty to 'pick and choose' from the scriptures what suits our

[1] H. G. Hageman, *Pulpit and Table*, III.

taste, and discard the rest. We must be concerned with the whole biblical basis of Christian worship, not with slavishly copying externals and methods, but with the recovery of basic insights and convictions. Not with the ways of doing it, but with the theology and principles implicit in the ways of doing it. In all ages the church has the dual task, both of seeking to understand afresh the essentials of the biblical revelation, and of applying these insights and convictions to contemporary circumstances and needs.

Having studied the Bible, we shall not then make 'the great leap' from the first century to the twentieth as if nothing of any significance had happened in between. 'The history of Christian worship is not that of a series of mistakes best forgotten; it has much to teach twentieth-century man, whether he be aware of it or not, and in an attempt to meet the contemporary situation the riches of former ages should not be neglected.'[1] There are distortions and errors as well as riches. Much can be learned both negatively and positively from the story of the church, for the reformation and enrichment of our worship today. No attempt will be made to outline the history of worship, but a selection of material relevant to the particular theme will be made from the history of the church whether before or after the Reformation. In the concluding part of each chapter, an attempt will be made to apply the biblical insights and lessons from church history to the worship of our churches today. To what extent is that worship already biblically grounded and theologically sound? What reforms are desirable or necessary, and what general direction should they take?

In this study, no attempt will be made to advocate or vindicate any one particular tradition of worship. No tradition should be regarded as exempt from constructive criticism in the light of ecclesiastical tradition as a whole, and the latter in turn must be subjected to the criticism of the prophetic and apostolic tradition enshrined in scripture. Unfortunately in no sphere are churches more conservative and resistant to change than in that of worship. Loyalty is so often given to what is in fact a relatively recent and bad tradition. Even the heirs of the Reformation can come to regard reformation as an event or series of events in the sixteenth century, rather than as a continuing, contemporary, dynamic and never-completed process. It is so easy to forget that the God we worship is 'on the side of that which is coming

[1] G. Cope, J. G. Davies, and D. A. Tytler, *An Experimental Liturgy*, 7–8.

into being'. But the true church, the covenant-people on pilgrimage, offering worship not in a fixed temple but in a movable tabernacle, will never cease to reform her worship under the inspiration and guidance of the Word and the Spirit of the living God.

Chapter II

WORSHIP AS DIALOGUE

1. Conversation with God

THE human body has a given structure. Is this also true of our worship? Is there a right 'order of service', from which we should not depart? Not all would agree that such is the case, and in some traditions the following three assumptions are widespread. A Christian service is comprised of a number of items. These may be arranged according to the inclination of the person conducting it. Like a pack of cards, the items may legitimately be re-shuffled for the next occasion. As over against these assumptions, it will be maintained in this chapter that Christian worship *has* a given structure, which arises out of God's encounter with men. The Bible itself is the record of that encounter, which through word and sacrament is continued in all ages. The nature of our worship is determined by the two sides or aspects of that personal encounter. It has the pattern of a dialogue, of revelation and response, of divine word and human answer. Here is one example of such a dialogue.

> 'Now the word of the Lord came to me saying,
> "Before I formed you in the womb I knew you, and before you were born I consecrated you; I appointed you a prophet to the nations."
> Then I said,
> "Ah, Lord God! Behold, I do not know how to speak, for I am only a youth."
> But the Lord said to me,
> "Do not say 'I am only a youth'; for to all to whom I send you you shall go, and whatever I command you you shall speak. Be not afraid of them, for I am with you to deliver you, says the Lord." '[1]

This account of the call of Jeremiah, which is no doubt the distilla-

[1] Jer. 1. 4–8.

tion of many years of reflection and experience, takes the form of a dialogue. God speaks, Jeremiah answers, and God speaks yet again. Not only the call, but also the subsequent ministry of this, the greatest of the Hebrew prophets, is an intimate dialogue with God. Here is encounter and conversation, revelation and response, God's word and man's answer. Enoch, who lived in intimate companionship with his maker, is said to have 'walked with God'.[1] This metaphor is revealing. When two friends go for a walk, they enter into fellowship through conversation. They are not necessarily talking all the time, for in the context of revealing conversation, communication can also take place through silence. For 'even when this communication is felt in silence, which we are fond of saying is more eloquent than speech, this silence is itself charged with the words that have been exchanged before it began'.[2] The spoken words, like the traffic on the highway, move in two directions. For not all the speaking is done by one of the two friends, and all the listening by the other. That of course can happen. A bore has been defined as 'a man who talks about himself when I want to talk about myself'! If, however, there is to be genuine communication, he who has spoken must also listen, and he who has been addressed must also speak. Conversation is dialogue, not monologue. Communion with God is a two-way conversation, in which God speaks and man answers.

God both speaks and listens. 'It is God's love for us that he not only gives us his Word, but also lends us his ear.'[3] In this chapter we shall study this dialogue in the worship of the Old and New Testaments. We shall then look at certain distortions of it in the history of the church, due first to a neglect of the preaching of the word and then to an extreme reaction in the opposite direction, which made inadequate provision for the human response. This will lead up to a discussion of the structure of our church worship today. What should be the pattern and content of our services and sacraments if our worship is to be a true encounter with God, a genuine dialogue of word and answer?

2. Three misunderstandings of the dialogue

Before turning to the Bible, reference must first be made to three widespread misunderstandings of the dialogue of worship. It is often

---

[1] Gen. 5. 24.   [2] P. Tournier, *The Meaning of Persons*, 130.
[3] D. Bonhoeffer, *Life Together*, 87.

assumed that the dialogue between God and man consists only, or mainly, of the exchange of spoken words. We lay ourselves open to this misunderstanding by using the analogy of human conversation. That is an illustration of *one* aspect of the divine-human encounter; it is not *only* in this sense that we are to understand revelation and response, God's word and man's answer. Today, as in the demand *facta non verba*, we are accustomed to make a contrast between words and deeds. If applied to God, such a contrast is false. For the word of God is God himself, active in creation and providence, in mercy and judgment, in revelation and redemption. God does his word. It is creative, active, dynamic; it achieves his purposes. 'So shall my word be that goes forth from my mouth; it shall not return to me empty, but it shall accomplish that which I purpose, and prosper in the thing for which I send it.'[1] Whether in the cult or in life, the word of God may be communicated through words, but it is always far more than words. Nor, on the other hand, must we limit the human response to spoken words. These indeed have a part, important and indispensable in worship; but the part is not the whole. The response may be action, accompanied or unaccompanied by words. In the sacrifices of the old covenant the praises and the prayers accompanied the gift and the action. The response was a union of word and deed. The dialogue between God and man is more closely analogous to the relationship between man and wife in marriage. It is a living communication in which word and deed, gift and service, mind and body all have part. God gives himself to his people in loving kindness and faithfulness. And the response which he requires is not merely verbal, but the oblation of the whole personality.

It is also misleading to draw too hard and fast a line between the downward movement of God to man, and the upward movement of man to God in the dialogue of worship. The two movements cannot be rigidly separated, and should not be regarded as either successive or mutually exclusive. It is indeed possible to analyse Christian worship and to distinguish the two movements. 'In this part of the service God is approaching, addressing, and giving himself to the worshippers, whereas in this part the worshippers are approaching, addressing, and giving themselves to God.' But such distinctions have relative, not absolute, validity. Intellectually the two movements may be dis-

[1] Isa. 55. 11.

tinguished; in the experience of worship they are closely intertwined and often merged. A hymn, for example, is a response, a spiritual sacrifice offered by the worshippers to God. It may also at the same time be used by God to address the worshippers. In worship, as in a conversation between two friends, there is constant interchange. The two movements are woven together, like the warp and woof of a garment.

We must also be on our guard against the error that God alone is active in the descending, and man alone active in the ascending movement of worship. For God is active in all true worship, which is impossible in either direction apart from the presence and activity of the Holy Spirit. God is indeed active in approaching and addressing man through his word; but here also man is active in reading, preaching, and obeying that word. The worshippers are indeed active in praise and prayer, in the offering of gifts and of themselves; but here also God is active, inspiring the response. Whether we are listening or speaking, receiving or offering, God is active in the Spirit. As regards prayer, this is how Lady Julian of Norwich put this truth into the mouth of God.

> 'I am the ground of thy beseeching.
> First, it is my will that thou have it,
> And then I make thee to will it,
> And then I make thee to beseech it.'

Both revelation and response depend upon the presence and activity of the Holy Spirit, the Lord and giver of life and light. This activity of God in both the ascending and descending movements, is finely described by Robert Will. 'In the phenomena of worship we see two currents of life meet, one proceeding from the transcendent Reality, the other flowing from the religious life of the subject; one descending, the other ascending. These two currents are not only to be recognized in the sacramental and sacrificial aspects of worship – the descending current includes all forms of revelation, the ascending, all forms of prayer. Nor does the mutual action of the two currents exclude the primacy of the divine action; for this is manifest not only in the descending current of the Word, of Revelation, and of sacramental action, but also in its immanent action within the life of souls.'[1]

[1] R. Will, *Le Culte*, II, 552.

3. Jacob's ladder

In the religion of the Bible as a whole 'mystery lives and moves in all its potency'.[1] The revelation of the mysterious and holy God calls forth from man the basic response of awe and wonder, a response of sentiment and action, as well as of spoken word. One of the best illustrations of this dialogue of revelation and response is the story of the encounter between God and Jacob at Bethel.[2] In his dream, the patriarch sees a stairway reaching up from earth to heaven. On this 'ladder' there is movement in two directions. The angels are ascending from earth to heaven and descending from heaven to earth. It is a vision of the two-way communication which is always taking place between God and men. Bending over him as he sleeps, God takes the initiative in revealing himself to Jacob. He speaks, promising to give to the fugitive the land on which he lies, and descendants without number. On waking from sleep Jacob reponds to this divine revelation. And here we see, as was stressed above, that the human 'answer' in worship is not merely verbal and rational. The basic response is emotional, for the dreadful, the mysterious, the holy, is baffling to the intelligence and far beyond its reach. Confronted with the numinous object, the *mysterium tremendum*, the complex emotion, the sentiment of awe is evoked. 'How awesome is this place!' Bearing in mind the divine promises made to him while asleep, Jacob also, no doubt, felt gratitude. And 'awe compounded with gratitude' is 'the highly compound emotion of *reverence*', a 'blend of wonder, fear, gratitude and negative self-feeling', the 'religious emotion *par excellence*'.[3] The response to revelation is a sentiment which issues in spoken word and sacramental act. He sets up a monolith, consecrates it with oil, and makes a vow. 'If God will be with me, and will keep me in this way that I go, and will give me bread to eat and clothing to wear, so that I come again to my father's house in peace, then the Lord shall be my God, and this stone which I have set up for a pillar shall be God's house; and of all that thou givest me I will give the tenth to thee.'[4] Here is revelation and response, message and prayer, divine promise and human vow, the sentiment of awe and sacramental act, symbol and

---

[1] R. Otto, *The Idea of the Holy*, 87.   [2] Gen. 28. 10–22.
[3] W. McDougall, *An Outline of Psychology*, 334.
[4] Gen. 28. 20–22.

sanctuary. Divine revelation, seen and heard, vision and message, elicits a response in which emotion, word, and action are combined.

It is no accident that the story of the encounter between God and Jacob at Bethel is told in picture language. 'The Bible, the book of the divine encounter, is *par excellence* the book of pictures and conversations. It describes God's age-long dialogue with men and provokes them to participate in that dialogue still.'[1] A distinguished physician and psychologist, Dr Paul Tournier, has drawn attention to the fact that image and metaphor, parable and story are the language of personal encounter. 'A thing that strikes me when I am talking with my patients is that the moment deep personal contact is made, the very style of our talk changes. Images spring spontaneously to the mind, we begin to talk in parables, and we understand one another better than when the tone of our conversation was intellectual and didactic.'[2] This is the language of the Bible and of the great liturgies.

4. The old covenant

From the story of Jacob at Bethel, we have illustrated the dialogue in terms of individual response to divine revelation. We turn now to the answer of the People of God to his word. This sequence is not meant to imply that the individual is prior to the people; personal and communal are correlative terms and there can be no answer to the question, 'which comes first?' The twofold movement in worship is clearly seen in the story of the ratification of the old covenant.[3] Redemption and revelation precede and are the background of this event. For God was already known as the redeemer of Israel. He had led the Hebrew slaves out of Egypt 'with a strong hand and an outstretched arm'; he had 'divided the Red Sea in sunder, and made Israel pass through the midst of it.'[4] The exodus was followed by a further revelation of his glory and a new disclosure of his demands at Mount Sinai 'in cloud and majesty and awe'. The people of God responded to this act of emancipation, and to this disclosure of his will and commandments, with submission and obedience. Moses came down from Sinai and entered the assembly bearing 'the words of the Lord.' He declared these to the people, and they responded, 'all the words which the Lord has spoken we will do'. Having received this obedient response, Moses

[1] T. H. Keir, *The Word in Worship*, 63.
[2] *The Meaning of Persons*, 132.
[3] Exod. 24. 3–8.
[4] Ps. 136. 12–14.

wrote down all the words of the Lord in a book. An altar was then erected, and stones representing the twelve tribes were set up round about it. At the command of Moses, the young men offered burnt offerings and sacrificed peace-offerings. In order to ratify the covenant, some of the blood of the victims was dashed against the stone altar, which represented the active presence of God. Before proceeding to include the people in the binding relationship, they were asked yet again to give assent to the words of the Lord, to accept the written obligations which were the basis of the covenant. They responded 'all that the Lord has spoken we will do, and we will be obedient.' The blood which ratified the covenant was then sprinkled on the people. God and Israel were bonded, both parties were joined together by the blood of the communal sacrifice. To the grace of the redeemer manifested in the exodus, and to the demands of the holy God revealed on Sinai, the people had responded with the promise of obedience. This old covenant established at Mount Sinai, after which Christians have named all the scriptures of Israel, is the type of which Christian worship is the antitype. Here is word and answer, redemption and revelation, book and preacher, prophet and priest, assembly and altar, sacrifice and sacrament, covenant and pledge. It is a dialogue foreshadowing the main elements of our Christian worship.

'Behind the people's national life lay the consciousness of redemption as much as it lies behind the life of the Christian.'[1] It is in the light of the exodus and of 'all the saving deeds of the Lord',[2] and from *within* the covenant established by his grace, that we must understand all the subsequent worship of the Old Testament. He who had redeemed his people from Egypt and established his covenant at Sinai, continued to act in deliverance and judgment, and to reveal his word through priest, prophet, and wise man. Through all three, for Jeremiah speaks of the *torah* of the priest, and the counsel of the wise, and the word of the prophet, as the three channels of revelation.[3] It is a popular misunderstanding to suppose that the original and primary function of the priest was to offer sacrifice. In the primitive period a layman could do that; but he went to the priest 'to enquire' of the Lord. 'For the lips of a priest should guard knowledge, and men should seek instruction from his mouth, for he is the messenger of the Lord of hosts.'[4] 'Levi is

---

[1] A. B. Davidson, 'God', in Hastings, *Dictionary of the Bible*, II, 202.
[2] 1 Sam. 12. 7.   [3] Jer. 18. 18.   [4] Mal. 2. 7.

primarily characterized by his possession of the sacred oracle, the urim and thummin. He teaches Israel Yahweh's *mishpatim* and *toroth*, and [in Deut. 33. 8–11] his sacrificial function is named last.'[1] The prophet, present at the council of God, must deliver the message entrusted to him. What God has revealed to him, he declares to Israel. He interprets the action of God in history. The maxims of the wise, although based on observation and experience, are also a channel of divine revelation. Directly through the oracles of the priests and the prophets, indirectly through the practical counsel of the wise men, God continued to address his Word to his people. The required response to this continuing divine word was obedience, expressed both in life and in ritual worship. The sacrifices, usually accompanied by praises and prayers, were the human response to the redemptive activity and revealed will of God. Whether offered in homage or gratitude, to fulfil a vow or obtain a petition, to establish fellowship or expiate sin, they presuppose the covenant which they strengthen or renew. Even in later times, when sacrifices were offered simply because the written law required them, they were still regarded as response in obedience to the revealed will of a gracious God. It is as a continuing dialogue that the worship of the Old Testament is seen in its true perspective.

5. Revelation and response in the new covenant

'When in former times God spoke to our forefathers, he spoke in fragmentary and varied fashion through the prophets. But in this final age he has spoken to us in the Son.'[2] The gospel is the story of God's self-disclosure in Christ; Christian life and worship is the answer. This revelation is a saving action. At the transfiguration, our Lord talked with Moses and Elijah about *the exodus* he was to accomplish at Jerusalem.[3] He who had emancipated the Hebrew slaves from Egypt was about to deliver the captives of sin and death, through the sacrifice and victory of his Son. Through this act of liberation God established the new Israel, ratifying the new covenant with the blood of Christ. As at Sinai, the people responded to the words of the Lord spoken by Moses, so we are invited through the lips of those who preach the gospel, to respond in the obedience of faith to the word made flesh, through whose sacrificed life the new bond is established.

[1] H. Wheeler Robinson, *Inspiration and Revelation in the Old Testament*, 201.
[2] Heb. 1. 1, 2. N.E.B.   [3] Luke 9. 31.

Only in the light of the incarnation can we fully understand the dialogue of worship. As was pointed out above, we must be on guard
against the assumption that the conversation between God and man
consists only or mainly in the exchange of spoken words. God does
indeed speak words to us through the lips of Jesus Christ. His teaching
and preaching is an essential part of the revelation. But the part is not
the whole. The word of God is a deed; the person of the Son of God
and his saving work is the content of the revelation. 'He has spoken to
us in the Son'. So also, our human answer to this word must be a total
response. Spoken words, especially of praise and thanksgiving, of prayer
and confession of the Name, have an essential place within this response.
The full response, like the word to which it is the answer, must be
made in deed, in obedience, in the life, in the flesh. Our spiritual worship is the offering of the whole personality in response to the mercies
of God in Christ.[1]

Now this oblation of the whole personality in response to the grace
of God in Christ, is focused within and made possible by those specific
acts of corporate *worship* to which we usually confine that word. The
nature of this response within the cultus is determined by the content
of the revelation. Three outstanding characteristics of the response may
be noted here. Christian worship is centred in Christ, it is rooted in
history, it is inspired by gratitude. It is Christocentric; as in heaven, so
on earth, the Lamb stands in the midst of the assembly at worship.[2]
Through Christ we have been redeemed, through Christ we know
God, through Christ we have access to the Father in one Spirit.[3]
Christian worship is both trinitarian and Christocentric. For it is
through the grace of our Lord Jesus Christ that we know the love of
God and have fellowship with him and with one another through the
presence and activity of the Holy Spirit.[4] In the foreground of the
worship of the New Testament is the grace of the eternal Son, just as its
terminus or goal is always the eternal Father. 'For we are the true circumcision, who worship by the Spirit of God *and glory in Christ Jesus.*'[5]

The word of God, Jesus Christ, to whom we respond in the dialogue
of worship, was manifested in history. The gospel is the sacred story
of 'all the saving deeds of the Lord', of the incarnation and birth of his
Son, of his ministry mighty in deed and word, of his sufferings and

[1] Rom. 12. 1.   [2] Rev. 5. 6.   [3] Eph. 2. 18.
[4] 2 Cor. 13. 14.   [5] Phil. 3. 3. R.S.V. margin.

death upon the cross, of his glorious resurrection and ascension. These interpreted acts, this good news, was at first transmitted orally by the apostles and ministers of the word. It was proclaimed in the local assembly by prophets and evangelists, pastors and teachers. Imbued with pentecostal enthusiasm and power, the speakers in the assembly transmitted revelation, knowledge, prophecy, and teaching.[1] In due course, as at the ratification of the old covenant, the spoken word was committed to writing. The worship of the synagogue with its readings and exposition of the law and the prophets, increasingly and enduringly influenced the development of Christian worship. The word was not only spoken but read. Through prophecy and law, epistle and gospel, as through the interpretation and exposition of scripture, the people were taken back to the historic acts of God in Christ; or rather, the saving events were made contemporary through the word. Rooted in history, Christian worship is scriptural. The saving events were also proclaimed and re-presented in the assembly through the sacraments. Through both word and sacrament, that which God had done in the past, was brought into the present. The word of God was spoken, enacted, made contemporary, in the worshipping assembly.

The Spirit inspired answer to the word declared in the assembly is gratitude. This found expression in psalms and hymns, in confessions of faith and exclamations of praise, in *glossolalia* and in prayer. This upward movement was fervent and enthusiastic, spontaneous and pentecostal. This gratitude came to full expression in the celebration of the Lord's Supper. Commemorating the death and resurrection of Christ, the People of God responded by offering the sacrifice of praise and thanksgiving. Primitive Christian worship was essentially eucharistic. It was the corporate exclamation – 'Thanks be to God for his inexpressible gift!'[2]

6. The dialogue distorted

In the history of the church, worship has not fully retained its character as dialogue. Owing to the intrusion of alien thought and influence, there has been a departure in various ways from 'the radical and consistent personalism' of the Bible. 'The Christian teaching about God and his relationship with man is personalistic through and through.'[3] It did not, however, always retain this character. The

---

[1] 1 Cor. 14. 6.   [2] 2 Cor. 9. 15.   [3] H. H. Farmer, *God and Men*, 33.

C

revelation of God was blurred and distorted when set forth in alien and impersonal categories of thought. The God of Abraham, Isaac, and Jacob, the God of the prophets and the apostles, the Father of our Lord Jesus Christ, was hidden away behind highly generalized statements and abstract language. Worship ceased to be personal encounter when it was no longer realized that 'knowing God is analogous to hearing and answering'.[1] For it is the living, personal God who speaks and requires an answer. How could he speak clearly in the assembly when the scriptures were no longer read audibly in the language of the people, and the preaching of the word was neglected? Where there was no word, there was no answer. The worshippers became mere spectators of a mysterious rite, performed by priestly experts, in which they had little or no part.

It is, however, with a distortion of a different kind that we are now concerned and one which is the background of our church situation in Britain. In the centuries following the Reformation, there was a marked tendency to distort the dialogue of worship, by laying too strong an emphasis upon one of its two aspects at the expense of the other. In this respect nonconformist and Anglican worship may be compared and contrasted. 'If, for convenient but not absolute purposes of description, a distinction can be made between the downward movement of revelation and the upward movement of aspiring, human response, then the Puritan cultus stressed the former and the Anglican cultus the latter.'[2] For the Puritans and their successors, the stress lay heavily, almost exclusively, upon the downward movement of God. Through the reading of the scriptures (at length) and the preaching of the word in the power of the Spirit, God was revealed and communicated to the worshippers. They assembled primarily in order to hear the word of God. Even the praises, the metrical psalms, were the word of God; and the long extempore prayers of the minister, usually offered from the pulpit, tended to be didactic, directed to the edification of the worshippers as well as to God. The lofty central pulpit dominating the chapel was itself a symbol of the centrality of the word. There was a tendency to regard all the other aspects of worship as 'the preliminaries' to the sermon. This is not to say that the Lord's Supper was regarded as unimportant. It was usually administered after careful

[1] J. S. Whale, *Christian Doctrine*, 55.
[2] Horton Davies, *Worship and Theology in England*, 32.

preparation, and with all due solemnity and devotion. Yet here also, a s in preaching, the emphasis was upon the divine word. The Lord's Supper was the *verbum visibile*, and the divine seal to the preaching of the gospel. The response to this word was to be made not in 'the service' but in life. Little emphasis was placed on worship as offering. Indeed there was often intense suspicion of, or open hostility to, the idea that the worshippers do or can offer anything to God. Even today, many Free Churchmen are reluctant to refer to 'the collection' as 'the offering'. In worship the God of all grace descends the stairway, as he is proclaimed by scripture, preacher, and ordinance. We can but receive him with gratitude and obey him in life.

It would, of course, be a serious misrepresentation to belittle the importance of the word of God in Anglican worship. In the Book of Common Prayer, Cranmer sought to ensure that the word should be read and preached at the celebration of holy communion. At Morning and Evening Prayer, in psalm and canticle, in Old and New Testament lections, the Bible is both read to the congregation and provides much of the language for the congregational response. But when these necessary qualifications have been made, it still remains true that the typical and central emphasis in Anglican worship is not upon the proclamation of the word of God, but rather upon the offering of worship by the people. There has been and still is a tendency among Anglicans to regard the sermon as a mere homily. At Morning and Evening Prayer it is not a part of the liturgy. On the other hand, the liturgy itself is highly valued, chiefly as a means of corporate praise and prayer. It enables the people to offer adoration and thanksgiving, penitence and intercession, together with all those using the liturgy in every place This offering is focused in the sacrament of the altar. Re-presenting and united with Christ's eternal sacrifice, the church, together with the sacrifice of praise and thanksgiving, offers herself to God. Not the pulpit and that which is proclaimed from it, but the altar and that which is offered upon it, is the centre of Anglican worship.

This contrast between 'chapel' and 'church' can easily be exaggerated or overdrawn. It is a matter of emphasis; an emphasis which needs to be corrected, not by belittling that which has been stressed, but by supplying the counter-emphasis. The pattern of Christian worship should reflect the dialogue between God and man as a balanced whole. Because the divine word has priority, the human answer must not be ignored or under-valued. For God speaks in order that we may offer ourselves. And must not *a part* of the response be made *within* the cultus itself? In the light of what we have seen of the dialogue in the Bible and in the history of the church, we turn now to study the pattern of our church worship today.

7. Dialogue in church worship

The structure of our church worship has been profoundly influenced by the tradition of the Jewish synagogue. Here the main element in the service was the reading and exposition of the scriptures. To this was added the sacred pattern of words and actions given to us by our Lord in the upper room, for the commemoration of his sacrifice until his advent in glory. Would it be true to designate these two main parts of our worship *Wort* and *Antwort*, revelation and response? Only in the sense that the main emphasis in the first part of the service is on the word of God, read and preached, whereas the main emphasis in the second part is on our response in adoration and thanksgiving, oblation and communion. It is important here to bear in mind the point made earlier in this chapter. It is not possible to draw a hard and fast line between the upward and downward movements in worship. Any such analysis has a relative, not an absolute validity. The great eucharistic prayer, the thanksgiving which consecrates, is an example of the impossibility of separating revelation and response, God's grace and man's offering. As *anamnesis*, as a memorial of the sacrifice of Christ, it declares the saving deeds of the Lord, who by his word and Spirit makes the bread we break and the cup over which we give thanks, to be the communion of the body and blood of Christ. On the other hand, as thanksgiving and oblation it is the climax of our human response. Accepting, then, this fact that our analysis has only a relative validity, and that in some cases it is largely a matter of emphasis, it is helpful to distinguish those aspects of worship in which God approaches, addresses, and gives himself to the people, from the parts in which the people approach, address, and give themselves to God. These interwoven strands of the dialogue can be analysed as follows:

THE PREPARATION

Word: The Call to Worship
Answer: The Prayer of Invocation

Answer: Psalm or Hymn of Praise
Word: The Call to Penitence
Answer: The Confession of Sin
Word: The Declaration of Pardon
Answer: The Prayer of Supplication

THE LITURGY OF THE WORD

Word: The Old Testament and the Epistle
Answer: The Psalm
Word: The Gospel
Word: The Sermon
Answer: The Creed or other Confession of Faith
Answer: Prayers of Intercession and Commemoration

THE LITURGY OF THE UPPER ROOM

Word: The Call to Give: Offertory Sentences
Answer: The Offertory of Bread, Wine, and Money: of Man's
Work
Word: The Invitation to the Lord's Table ('The Comfortable
Words') and the Words of Institution ('The Warrant')
Word and
Answer: The Eucharistic Prayer: Adoration – Thanksgiving – Mem-
orial – Invocation of the Spirit – Oblation
Word: The Breaking of Bread: the repetition of the Lord's words
and actions with the Bread and the Cup
Answer: The Communion: the Reception of Christ
Answer: The Thanksgiving for Communion
Answer: Hymn: Act of Praise or Dedication
Word: The Blessing of God

This pattern raises some important questions about the present ordering of our church worship. Why do we not complete the liturgy of the
word with the liturgy of the upper room every Lord's day? Why, on
most Sundays of the year, should we withhold the full diet of Christian worship from our congregations? We shall revert to this question
again. Here, we are concerned with another, although closely allied,
question. In those services in which the word is not followed by the
sacrament, should the main prayers of the congregation precede or

follow the preaching? It has long since become the general and established custom in both Anglican and Free Church services (other than the holy communion) to conclude the service with sermon, hymn, and benediction. In justification of this order, it is maintained that preaching is the true climax of worship, and that God should be allowed to have the last word. The true response of the people to the word of God is obedience in daily life. It is well for us, therefore, to go forth with the divine message ringing in our ears. There are, however, serious objections to such a pattern of worship. In the dialogue between God and man, whether in life or within the cultus, the divine word has priority. The worship of man within the cultus, and his service beyond it, is the response, the answer. This truth ought to find expression and embodiment in the structure of our church worship. This, as is evident from Justin Martyr's *Apology*,[1] was the pattern of worship in the early church, and is in accordance with primitive reformed practice. After the preparatory praise and confession, we hear the word of God in scripture and sermon. Responding to his glory and grace, to his revealed will and purpose, to his message addressed to us in our own situation, we confess our faith, give thanks, make intercession, and offer the gifts which represent our daily work, together with our lives. Such a pattern provides the congregation with a more ample opportunity of responding to God through Christ within the service itself. Furthermore, the reading and preaching of the word in the power of the Spirit enlightens the mind, kindles the affections, stirs the will. The people are moved and inspired to offer themselves more worthily and wholeheartedly in confession of faith, in prayer, and in gift. God's word evokes man's answer.

Such a pattern has the additional merit of keeping the main parts of the word of God in close proximity. In the now familiar order of service, the reading of the lesson or lessons is widely separated by hymns and prayers, notices and offering, from the preaching of the word. But the word, read and spoken, should be one whole, since preaching is the declaration of the living word *from the written word* by the spoken word. There is therefore great gain when the lections from the Old and New Testaments, or from epistle and gospel, are followed almost immediately by the sermon. Such a practice would tend to discourage the kind of preaching which has little relationship to the Bible.

[1] *First Apology*, c. 65–67.

The dialogue of worship has a bearing also upon the architecture and plan of the church building. While it is not of primary importance, it is certainly helpful to have one place from which the word is proclaimed, and another from which the congregational response of prayer is offered. If the prayers are said from the pulpit facing the congregation, the impression may be given that, as in reading and preaching, the minister is still addressing the congregation. The lectern and the pulpit are the throne of the word; here God speaks through reader and preacher to the people. Prayer should be offered at the Lord's Table, or from a desk in the front at right-angles to the congregation. Where there is a central aisle, for the main prayers the minister may kneel or stand in the midst of the congregation, facing in the same direction. It is not ideal that the choir should face the people when praises are being offered up to God. Only those who contrast, in unbiblical fashion, the inner and the outer, lay all the stress on the former and belittle the latter, will despise such aids to the appreciation of the dialogue of worship.

8. Dialogue in the sacraments

The nature of worship as dialogue should be patent not only in the liturgy of the word, with its readings and preaching, its praises and prayers, but also in the celebration of the gospel sacraments of baptism and the eucharist. For, as was stressed above, the dialogue between God and man does not consist only or mainly in the exchange of spoken words. Jacob did as well as said something in response to divine revelation and promise. God ratified the spoken and written words of the old covenant with sacrificial blood. When the time had fully come, the word became flesh, was manifested in mighty deeds as well as in words, and offered himself an unblemished sacrifice to God. The grace and truth of God is mediated in the assembly not only through spoken words, but also through the actions which accompany the words and are interpreted by them. The Lord acts through that which is done by his people with water, and with bread and wine, in obedience to his ordinances. There is no justification for the unexamined but widespread assumption that God acts through the spoken words of his servants, but not through that which they do with matter. Why this prejudice against matter which God created? We are not Gnostics, Manichaeans, or Christian Scientists. So also the response of the worshippers to the spoken and enacted word of God may itself be both something said and something done. Baptism and the eucharist are both said and done, in obedience to Christ's commands, through the inspiration of the Holy Spirit. As our bodies are washed with pure water, as we break the bread and bless the cup, we are responding in word and deed to the word of God, incarnate, crucified, risen, exalted. Only when the sacraments are understood in terms of personal encounter, dialogue, can the nature of sacramental grace be rightly understood. 'It is no new thought, but it cannot be too often before our eyes, that the grace offered in baptism, as in the eucharist, is no impersonal influence, injected through material substances, but *the gracious action of God himself.*'[1] In both sacraments, God meets us through Christ in the Spirit, and calls for the response of repentance, faith, and allegiance. Both alike are intended to be encounter, word and answer.

Baptism is the sacrament of the word of God. This has already been spoken to the catechumen through the preaching and teaching of the gospel in the power of the Holy Spirit. Having been born anew through 'the good news which was preached . . . the living and abiding word of God',[2] the catechumen is responding in repentance, faith, and promise, to this initiative of God through the gospel and the Spirit. The baptismal rite itself is both spoken and enacted word. The *kerygma*, 'that Christ died for our sins in accordance with the scriptures, that he was buried, that he was raised on the third day in accordance with the scriptures',[3] is here proclaimed and embodied. To this whole action of God in the Spirit through the gospel and in baptism, the catechumen responds in the renunciation of sin, the confession of faith, and the promise of allegiance.

Question: Do you renounce sin and all teachings and practices which you know to be contrary to God's will?

Answer: I renounce them.

Question: Do you believe in one God, the Father, the Son, and the Holy Spirit?

Answer: I believe.

Question: Do you accept Jesus Christ as your Lord and Saviour?

Answer: I do.

[1] G. R. Beasley-Murray, *Baptism in the New Testament*, 265. Italics his.
[2] I Peter I. 25, 23.   [3] I Cor. 15. 3, 4.

Question: Do you promise to follow Christ and serve and obey him in the fellowship of his church?

Answer: I promise.

This is the YES, the AMEN, the human response to the love of God in Christ crucified and risen, inspired by the Holy Spirit. It is the supreme manifestation of the radical personalism of our faith. Only in this context of dialogue can baptism be rightly understood and practised.

As the Passover was a proclamation by action of the exodus, so the eucharist is a proclamation by action of the new and greater exodus, the sacrifice and victory of Christ. The verb commonly used elsewhere in the New Testament of the proclamation of the gospel is used also of the Lord's Supper. 'For as often as you eat this bread and drink the cup, you *proclaim* the Lord's death until he comes.'[1] The eucharist is the *verbum visible*, the enacted word. He who is thus proclaimed is present within the assembly, doing that which he has commanded. The *anamnesis* is not the mental recollection of a past event or an absent person; it is the re-presentation of an immortal sacrifice, of a risen and present Lord. 'Blessed be he *who comes* in the name of the Lord! Hosanna in the highest!'[2] He who rode in triumph into Jerusalem comes afresh in every eucharist and is greeted now as then. The loaf which we break and the cup over which we give thanks to God, are a joint-participation in the life of him who has passed through death. Eucharist is encounter because Christ is present; he who is proclaimed arrives in the assembly and enters our hearts. Our response is thanksgiving, oblation, and communion. We offer praise and thanksgiving, we present ourselves a living sacrifice, we feed upon him by faith. He comes and gives himself; in gratitude we receive him and offer ourselves. 'Behold, I stand at the door and knock; if anyone hears my voice and opens the door, I will come in to him and eat with him, and he with me.'[3] This is the dialogue of the eucharist.

9. Real worship is meeting

It is important that Christian congregations should be taught to understand worship as dialogue. Going to church can so easily degenerate from personal encounter to mere habit. The 'means of grace'

[1] I Cor. 11. 26.   [2] Matt. 21. 9.   [3] Rev. 3. 20.

may cease to be means and become ends in themselves. This is true especially of sermon and sacrament, the two most popular ecclesiastical idols. Enjoyment of the sermon can be a substitute for hearing and obeying the word of the Lord. 'And lo, you [the preacher] are to them like one who sings love songs with a beautiful voice and plays well on an instrument, for they hear what you say, but they will not do it.'[1] So too the aesthetic appreciation of the sacrament as a rite, can take the place of encounter with God in trust and commitment. Martin Buber has taught us that 'real life is meeting'; the same may be said of real worship. Mr Christopher Dawson remarked to Dr J. H. Oldham 'that he wasn't sure that he liked the phrase, "real life is meeting", because it suggested such an awful thought, if you put an 's' at the end of it.'[2] Perhaps we multiply our religious meetings in order to avoid *the* meeting, the meeting which we both desire and dread. Let us then go to the assembly with the right intention, to keep tryst, to meet God. 'There I will meet with you . . . I will speak with you.'[3] We go to church to meet with God, and to listen to what he has to say to us through scripture and preaching. 'In the living thought of the church the action of preaching is clearly understood to involve an encounter with God.' That it is this, and not merely the transmission of a deposit of ideas, is shewn by the form of the solemn bidding which introduces lections and sermon in the service of the reformed churches. The bidding is: 'Hear the Word of God'. Not 'read it' but 'hear it'.[4] If, however, both sides of the dialogue are to be preserved, the worshippers must not only listen to the Lord God, they must also speak *to him* in praise and prayer. Writing to Trajan of the worship of the early Christians, Pliny says 'they sang a hymn *to* Christ as God'. Do we sing our hymns *to* the Lord? Or do we perhaps sing them to ourselves? As in the questionable practice of 'community hymn singing', they are nowadays often taken out of the context of the dialogue, and sung because they give 'uplift' to the worshippers. Sometimes even the prayers are addressed not to God, but to the congregation; they are sermonettes really intended, in spite of their outward form, to teach, edify, or inspire. 'The American newspaper reporter who ironically commended "the best prayer ever offered to a Boston audience", said more than he knew.'[5] This is to turn

[1] Ezek. 33. 32.   [2] J. H. Oldham, *Life is Commitment*, 28.
[3] Exod. 25. 22.   [4] T. H. Keir, *The Word in Worship*, 1.
[5] R. Abba, *Principles of Christian Worship*, 87.

prayer into a kind of dumb-bell exercise, a group form of what Charles Kingsley described as 'praying to oneself to change oneself; by which I mean the common method of trying by prayer to excite oneself into a state, a frame, an experience'. Dr H. E. Fosdick, who quotes these words, contrasts the prayer resolve of John Wesley, preserved on the first page of his numerous diaries, 'to converse *kata theon* – face to face with God'.[1] As with praises and prayers, so gifts also should be offered to God. Righteous Abel did not bring his gifts to the altar to support a worthy cause, or even to help the needy. Whatever use is subsequently made of the gifts, in worship they should be offered to God, as tokens of the oblation of ourselves. Worship is truly objective and not merely subjective, when it is addressed to God. He speaks to us; we speak to him. He gives himself to us; we give ourselves to him. Real worship is meeting.

On the façade of the Abbey at Bath, Jacob's ladder is carved in stone. As already suggested, this is the best symbol of the nature of worship as dialogue. Now in the Gospel of John, Jacob's ladder is identified with, or rather superseded by, our Lord Jesus Christ. 'Truly, truly I say to you, you will see heaven opened, and the angels of God ascending and descending *upon the Son of man*.'[2] 'John . . . reflecting upon the meaning of the incarnation, sees in Jesus, the Son of man, not merely an eschatological but an eternal contact between heaven and earth, God and man, and uses the ladder and the ascending and descending angels to express his conception.'[3] It is through him that the descending and ascending movements in Christian worship take place. God approaches us, and we approach God, through Christ. Through him the divine messages and blessings, and our human praises and prayers, are mediated. 'The Messiah himself is the meeting point of human need and divine blessing or judgment.'[4] The dialogue takes place through the 'one Mediator between God and men, the man Christ Jesus'.[5] The worship of the new covenant, in both directions, is 'through Jesus Christ our Lord'.

[1] H. E. Fosdick, *The Meaning of Prayer*, 31, 34.   [2] John 1. 51.
[3] C. K. Barrett, *The Gospel According to St John*, 156.
[4] W. Temple, *Readings in St John's Gospel*, 31.   [5] 1 Tim. 2. 5.

Chapter III

WORSHIP AS OFFERING

1. A lost emphasis

WORSHIP is offering. Without any explanation we are confronted at the very beginning of the Bible with the rite of sacrifice. Cain and Abel were the sons of Adam and Eve. 'In the course of time Cain brought to the Lord an offering of the fruit of the ground, and Abel brought of the firstlings of his flock and of their fat portions.'[1] These products of agricultural and pastoral life were offered up to the Lord on altars of stone. God accepted the gifts of the righteous Abel offered in faith,[2] and rejected the gifts of Cain. Perhaps the spirit and disposition of Cain, his jealousy and malice, was the cause of the rejection. Here, in the very first act of worship described in the Bible as now arranged, we have vegetable offering and animal sacrifice. The vital relationship between work and worship and the emphasis on right intention are also evident. For the products of toil – first fruits and firstlings – were offered; and yet it was not only the outer gift that was important, but also the inner intention or spirit in which it was offered. This incident is typical of the character of biblical worship. Not that the rite of sacrifice originated among the Hebrews. Ancient peoples in all parts of the world erected altars and offered sacrifices. The custom is primitive and universal. In the Bible, sacrifice as the sum of worship is found in a variety of forms. Before the tabernacle in the wilderness, on the high places in Canaan, in the courts of the temple at Jerusalem, to worship was to offer. 'Ascribe to the Lord the glory due his name; bring an offering, and come into his courts.'[3] The temple and priesthood of the new covenant, like that of the old, has also been built to offer sacrifices.[4] But this is a lost emphasis in much of our protestant worship today. 'Getting a blessing' has replaced 'making an offering'. There are many reasons for this change of emphasis. The perfect sacrifice of Christ, offered once for all, has abrogated and superseded the sacrifices of the old covenant. It is therefore wrongly assumed that

[1] Gen. 4. 3, 4.   [2] Heb. 11. 4.   [3] Ps. 96. 8.   [4] 1 Peter 2. 5.

Christian worship is no longer sacrificial. The Christian, it is maintained, cannot and need not offer any sacrifice to God; it has already been done for him. The prophetic criticism of the corrupt cultus has been misinterpreted to mean that the prophets were against sacrifices as such, and the prophetic element in the Old Testament has been emphasised at the expense of the priestly. The misinterpretation of the eucharist as in some sense a repetition of the sacrifice of Calvary, has itself resulted in an extreme reaction against the whole conception of worship as sacrifice. The almost exclusive stress of the Puritans and their successors on the downward movement in worship, upon the revelation and communication of God through the word, led to the virtual exclusion of the upward movement, the response, the offering of the worshippers. 'Let all things be done for edification.'[1] This Pauline saying was individualized and stressed apart from the Petrine reason for such corporate edification – 'be yourself built into a spiritual house, to be a holy priesthood, to offer spiritual sacrifices acceptable to God through Jesus Christ'.[2] The community is edified to offer, but the means was made the end, and the end itself ignored. For these various reasons, we have largely lost the conviction that worship is offering. In what follows, we shall look first at sacrifice in the Old and New Testaments, before considering how to give more adequate expression to this element in our worship today. No attempt will be made to distinguish offering and sacrifice. It is of course true that, while all sacrifices are offerings, not all offerings are sacrifices. The fruits brought by Cain were an offering, the animals brought by Abel a sacrifice. A sacrifice is an altar-offering, involving the death of an animal or human victim. But as soon as language is used metaphorically, this distinction can no longer be maintained. The money gifts of the Philippians were 'a fragrant offering, a sacrifice acceptable and pleasing to God'.[3] Sometimes in the Old Testament, the phrase 'sacrifice and offering' has reference to the animal and cereal types respectively. Usually, however, the words are employed synonymously, a convenient way of referring to altar-offerings in general.

2. The reasons of the heart

Why did the Israelites offer sacrifices to God? What was the purpose of these costly gifts, and what did they expect to achieve by offering

---

[1] I Cor. 14. 26.   [2] I Peter 2. 5.   [3] Phil. 4. 18.

them? We must be on our guard here against the errors of intellectualization and over-simplification. It would be contrary to all that we
know of the outlook and mentality of the Hebrews, to suppose that
they had a *rationale* of sacrifice, a theory of its nature and efficacy.
Probably the ancient worshipper was but dimly aware, if at all, of the
reasons for what he was doing. It is pertinent here to recall the memor-
able saying of Pascal, 'Le coeur a ses raisons.' The youth and the maid
do not give reasons why they have fallen in love. From the heart 'flow
the springs of life',[1] and the heart includes instinct and impulse, emotion
and intuition, intellect and will. To base sacrifice on intellect, or on a
universal instinct, is an over-simplification; it originates from *the whole*
personality of man responding to God. When, at a more reflective
stage, reasons are given or suggested, they are various and complex.
We must therefore resist the temptation to supply some *one* reason why
a sacrifice was offered. Even the same type was not necessarily offered
with the same intention. They all alike have one thing in common;
they are costly gifts to God. But a gift can be offered for a variety of
reasons. Made to a superior, it may be simply an expression of homage,
a token of respect or reverence, a dutiful act of obedience. Sometimes,
the gift was offered to discharge a vow made in a moment of spiritual
exaltation or deep distress. The 'sacrifice of thanksgiving' was an expression of gratitude for favour already received. Other sacrifices were
petitionary, the gift being accompanied by prayer for help or for suc-
cess in some endeavour. 'A gift is an invitation to friendship'; it can
create fellowship, or express and strengthen it where it already exists.
The sacrificial gifts gave expression to the communion already existing
between God and the worshippers, and thereby renewed and strengthened it. On the other hand, if that communion had been marred,
interrupted, or broken, sacrifice was offered as a means of expiating
the sin of the worshipper. As with gifts made by man to man, a sacrifice might be offered to procure favour or appease anger. In later times,
the predominant motive was that of obedience to the requirements of
the Torah. Nor must we overlook the deep impulse of the human
heart to express meaning in action. Although usually accompanied by
spoken words, by prayers or by songs, the sacrifices gave utterance in
the more eloquent language of action, to the deep desires, needs, and
aspirations of the heart of the worshipper. The mere recital of these

---

[1] Prov. 4. 23.

various reasons of the heart may serve to correct our almost inveterate modern tendency to equate sacrifice and sin – a point to which we must return presently. Sacrifice was offered for a variety of reasons, and these 'reasons' are of 'the heart', which according to Hebrew thought includes 'the head'.

3. The three main types

Amid all the varieties, there are three *main* types of sacrifice in the Old Testament. They are the peace offering, the burnt offering, and the sin offering. Of these, the first and the second are characteristic of the pre-exilic, the third of the post-exilic period.

The peace offering was a primitive act of worship, going far back into the nomadic period. It was sacrifice followed by a communal meal. Saul, searching for the lost asses of his father Kish, was present at such a sacred feast the day before he was anointed king.[1] Some time before Saul and his servant reached the guest hall, the headmen of Ramah had taken the animal victim to the high place outside the city and had killed it. The blood had been returned to God, poured out upon or at the foot of the altar. Certain fat portions of the victim were then burned upon the altar as an offering to God, and the flesh was prepared for the worshippers. Samuel and Saul shared in the meal in 'the hall' at the high place, with 'about thirty persons', the elders of the local community. It is unlikely that the Hebrews retained the primitive idea that God and the worshippers were literally sharing the same meal. 'It is rather more probable that the common eating of the group is the increase and sustenance of their strength and welfare as a group, family or cultic or both, by partaking in the presence of God ("before him") of a victim sanctified to him, whose life-force has been set free, sanctified by application of the blood to the altar, and released for the benefit of the worshippers.'[2] The peace offering was essentially a communion sacrifice, a joyful social or domestic occasion, at which the worshippers 'ate and drank before God'.

In the case of the burnt offering, the whole victim was given to God and consumed upon the altar. The fact that the entire gift was handed over to God, enhanced its value, and made this type of sacrifice especially appropriate for a solemn occasion. The men of Beth Shemesh

---

[1] I Sam. 9. 11–24.

[2] 'Sacrifice and Offering', in Hastings, *Dictionary of the Bible*, Second Edition, 870.

offered a sacrifice of this kind to celebrate the return of the Ark of God from the Philistines to Israel.[1] The two milch cows drawing the new cart which carried the ark came to a halt in the field of Joshua the Bethshemshite. The men of Beth Shemesh, having set up a great stone for an altar, split the wood of the cart for fuel 'and offered the cows as a burnt offering to the Lord'. It was an act of thanksgiving, a eucharist. This was a gift no part of which was taken back for the use of the worshippers; it was handed over entirely to God and consumed by fire. This was the oblation – the complete, the whole, the total gift.

The third type was the sin offering. Here the concern of the worshipper was the expiation of sin. Not of deliberate or wilful sin, for which no sacrifice could avail, but for unintentional offences against the holiness of God. One example maybe given from the Levitical codes.[2] A priest who has sinned unwittingly brings a bull without blemish to the altar, lays his hand upon it, and kills it. Taking some of the blood into the holy place, he sprinkles it with his finger seven times before the veil, and applies some of it to the horns of the altar of incense. The rest of the blood he pours out at the base of the altar of sacrifice. Having burned certain fat portions of the victim upon the altar, the rest of the flesh is carried outside the camp and burned. In this type of offering, which probably long antedates, but only comes into prominence after, the exile, the essential element was the offering of the blood, the life released by death. This had cleansing and sanctifying power, and was an expiation for involuntary or inadvertent sin.

These three main types of sacrifice express three fundamental needs and aspirations of man in relationship to God. The true worshipper longs for intimate communion with God, aspires to give himself wholly to God, and needs to be pardoned and cleansed by God. To these three basic needs and aspirations the three main types of sacrifice correspond – the peace offering, communion; the burnt offering, consecration; the sin offering, atonement.

4. The essentials of sacrifice

Three essential truths about the nature of sacrifice in the old covenant may be mentioned here, because of their bearing on the doctrines of the atonement and the eucharist, and upon Christian worship in general.

[1] 1 Sam. 6. 10–16.   [2] Lev. 4. 1–12.

The first concerns the material of sacrifice. What was the worshipper to offer to God? He was required to offer that which was his own, and which was for that reason precious to him. He was not enjoined to offer game or fish, the wild animals or creatures which belonged to God already. He must give that which was in a special sense his own. From the vegetable kingdom the worshipper was required to offer cereals, fruit, wine, oil; the constituents of his own daily food. The victim for the animal sacrifice was to be selected from the flock or the herd. The material for sacrifice had to be taken from the common life. It is true, of course, that whatever man gives to God belongs to him already. 'For all things come from thee, and of thy own have we given thee.'[1] On the other hand, in a relative but not an absolute sense, some things belong to a man, a family, a community, and others do not. All things in a household may belong to the father, but the children have their own clothes, books, pens, bicycles. The worshipper is to give to God that which in this special sense belongs to him, and is of value to him. The gift must be costly and precious. David would not accept as a gift the agricultural implements and the oxen which the Jebusite farmer offered to him for the sacrifice, because they did not belong to him but to Araunah. 'No, but I will buy it of you *for a price*; I will not offer burnt offerings to the Lord my God which *cost me nothing*.'[2] Not that the price could always be paid in money; the victim was often of value for another reason. 'The farmer who offered an unblemished sacrifice to his God had to choose from the herd an animal which he knew, so to speak, by a pet name, which had been a part of the family, and which was not only valuable to him but to some extent dear to him.'[3] The true sacrifice is never a substitute for self-offering; it is the costly surrender of that which is precious and dear, and, as such, an essential part of the self. The intention of Abraham to offer his own son, his only son, as a burnt offering, is (with the exception of Isaiah 53) the supreme example in the Old Testament of the meaning of sacrifice.[4]

In the second place, sacrifice must be associated with life and not primarily with death. It is life released through death and offered to God. In the mind of many Christians today, there is the misleading equation, sacrifice equals death. That which to the ancient Hebrews

---

[1] I Chron. 29. 14. [2] 2 Sam. 24. 24.
[3] N. Micklem, 'Leviticus', in *The Interpreter's Bible*, II, 11.
[4] Gen. 22. 1–12.

D

was a means to an end, the killing of the victim, has by us been regarded as an end in itself. Yet, in fact, the death of the victim was incidental; it was the means whereby the blood, the life, was released for offering to God. 'For the life of the flesh is in the blood; and I have given it for you upon the altar to make atonement for your souls; for it is the blood that makes atonement, by reason of the life.'[1] What was offered to God was 'sacrificed life', the life which had passed through death. This truth, that sacrifice was both the death of the victim *and* the offering of its life, is clearly seen in the ritual of the Day of Atonement.[2] The Aaronic priest was bidden to sacrifice a bull as a sin offering for himself, and a goat as a sin offering for the people. Having slain the victims, he bathed, put on his priestly vestments, and amid a cloud of incense entered the holy of holies. The blood of the bull and of the goat he sprinkled on the mercy-seat, the golden lid of the ark, and seven times before it. The sacrifice must not be identified with the first, but with both acts of the drama. It was offering to God life, which had first been released and made available through death. Sacrifice is '*life offered* in order that life may be received'.[3]

This definition leads on to the third truth, the sacramental nature of the sacrifices. Life was offered to God in order that life might be received from God. But was life in fact received through the sacrifices of the old covenant? Were they efficacious? Did the peace offering bring the worshippers into fellowship with God? Did the sin offering really take away sin? Were the sacrifices and offerings means of grace? An easy way to answer this question is to quote the Epistle to the Hebrews. 'For it is impossible that the blood of bulls and goats should take away sins.'[4] The ancient sacrifices were but shadowy anticipations of the one, full, perfect, and sufficient sacrifice of Christ, 'himself the Victim and himself the Priest'. It is, however, easy to draw wrong conclusions from this incontestable truth. There is no salvation for anyone in any age apart from the one sacrifice of Christ the redeemer. But does that sacrifice avail for men only in the ages after A.D. 30? Is there not a sense in which the sacrifices of the old covenant, like the sacraments of the new covenant, are related to the sacrifice of Christ and have validity because of it? Did not God forgive, cleanse, renew, strengthen,

---

[1] Lev. 17. 11.   [2] Lev. 16. 1–34.
[3] E. O. James, *Origins of Sacrifice*, 256. Italics mine.
[4] Heb. 10. 4.

and sanctify men of faith *in view of* the merits of Christ the Saviour of the world? In spite of the fragmentary and partial nature of the revelation, we affirm with the apostle Peter, that the Spirit of Christ was at work in the prophets of the old covenant.[1] Was he not also at work in the consecrated priest and the devout worshipper, receiving the gifts offered in faith and making them the channels of his grace? H. Wheeler Robinson has suggested that the ancient sacrifices are analogous to the symbolic acts of the Hebrew prophets. 'These acts, such as the wearing of a yoke or the breaking of pottery by Jeremiah, or Isaiah's walking about Jerusalem bare-foot and lightly clad, are more than dramatic expressions of what the prophet has otherwise said, simply expressing bondage, destruction, or captivity. Like the spoken word, they are instrumental acts, helping to bring about that which they signify. They are part of the divine activity, that part which the prophets initiate . . . The sacrifices also were symbolic acts, actualized approaches to God, which initiated a new relation to him for the group or the individual, when offered with the right intention.'[2] The sacrifices were instrumental symbols, sacramental acts. God used the gifts he himself had inspired and ordained, to mediate his presence and power, his forgiveness and grace, to the worshippers. The offerings of men were the sacraments of God.

5. A different emphasis

The Book of Common Prayer defines a sacrament as 'an outward and visible sign of an inward and spiritual grace'. The Bible does not thus distinguish the material and the spiritual, or contrast the outer and the inner. We do great injustice to the sacrificial worship of Israel if we regard it as concerned primarily with externals. The worshipper was himself identified with the offering, his inner attitudes found expression in the tangible gift from the vegetable or animal kingdom. We misrepresent the cult if this inner content is overlooked. Leviticus should be read in conjunction with the Psalter. The rubrics should not be separated from the liturgy; the directions on how to do it, and what you say as you do it, belong together. If the book of Leviticus is the bony skeleton, the prayers and praises and the 'glad shouts and songs of thanksgiving' of the Psalter, are the flesh and blood of the cult. We

---

[1] 1 Peter 1. 11.
[2] *Redemption and Revelation*, 250, 251.

misrepresent the worship of Israel if we think of the sacrifices apart
from the prayers and the songs, the intentions and the vows, the gratitude and the awe, the joy and the fellowship, which accompanied
them. However, this ideal unity of inner attitude and outer embodiment was not always maintained. It is perilously easy for acts of devotion to become mere acts devoid of devotion, for ritual to degenerate
into the 'dead routine of the legal sacrifices'.[1] Instead of expressing the
reverence and loyalty of the heart, the offerings and sacrifices could and
did become substitutes for true piety, personal obedience, and social
righteousness. Reference has already been made in chapter I to the
prophetic protest against this substitution. There it was maintained that
Amos, Hosea, Micah, Isaiah, and Jeremiah were protesting against the
corruption, the perversion of the cult (the substitution of costly offerings for holy living), and not against sacrificial worship as such. Never-
theless, there is undoubtedly a significant change of emphasis in these
prophets and in some of the psalmists. While they were not contending
for a 'purely spiritual' religion, they did put the stress on the heart
rather than on the cult, upon conduct rather than offering. Thus Hosea
invites the people to return to the Lord, but not with lambs, rams, or
bulls. 'Take with you *words* and return to the Lord; say to him "Take
away all iniquity; accept that which is good and we will render the
fruit of our lips".'[2] The cult of the word is preferred to the cult of the
altar. In place of bulls they are required to offer the bulls of the lips.
The penitent people are to approach God with words, with the liturgy
of confession, with 'the fruit of lips that acknowledge his name'.[3] Here
the stress is upon true penitence expressed in prayer, to the relative
disparagement of sacrificial worship. The psalmist,[4] grateful for deliverance from sickness and death, acknowledges that God does not
require a literal sacrifice of thanksgiving. Instead, he will offer himself
in whole-hearted obedience. 'Thou hast given me an open ear [literally,
'ears thou hast dug for me'] I delight to do thy will, O my God.'[5] It is
doubtful if the psalmist is saying that God does not require sacrifices at
all, but he certainly does not require them apart from the obedience of
the heart. The latter is what really matters. Obedience is better than
sacrifice, and is the best way of expressing gratitude. Kindness to others
is also the equivalent of, and perhaps superior to, sacrifice. 'By loyalty

---

[1] G. Adam Smith, *The Twelve Prophets*, I, 369.
[2] Hosea 14. 2.   [3] Heb. 13. 15.   [4] Ps. 40.   [5] Ps. 40. 6, 8.

and faithfulness iniquity is atoned for.'[1] Later on this same claim is made for charity or philanthropy. 'For almsgiving delivers from death, and it will purge away every sin.'[2] This significant shift of emphasis from the animal sacrifices to the 'spiritual sacrifices' of prayer, penitence, thanksgiving, obedience, kindness, and charity, is fulfilled in the new covenant. It is, however, an emphasis which can itself become one-sided. For man is not pure spirit, and the inner attitude and the outward form belong together. This tension can be seen in Psalm 51. The psalmist knows that God has no delight in animal sacrifices. 'The sacrifice acceptable to God is a broken spirit; a broken and contrite heart, O God, thou wilt not despise.'[3] But this revolutionary stress on a 'purely spiritual' devotion is corrected at the conclusion of the psalm. 'Do good to Zion in thy good pleasure; rebuild the walls of Jerusalem, then wilt thou delight in right sacrifices, in burnt offerings and whole burnt offerings; then bulls will be offered on thy altar.'[4] Verse 19 ('then wilt thou delight in right sacrifices') clearly contradicts verse 16, 'for thou hast no delight in sacrifice'. These concluding verses (18 and 19) are generally regarded, with insufficient evidence, as a later addition. Here 'the priest tones down the strong language of the prophet'[5] and corrects the impression left by verses 16 and 17 that God requires only spiritual sacrifices. The correction is significant and preserves the balance found in the Old Testament as a whole. Amos and Isaiah are succeeded by Haggai and Malachi, the prophets of the restored temple and cult. 'Forms of religion are still necessary even for the most spiritual worshippers.'[6]

6. The sacrifice of Christ

The scriptures of the new covenant are dominated throughout by the death and resurrection of Jesus Christ the Son of God. This event, climactic and crucial in the gospels, is interpreted in the epistles by means of several metaphors. The death and resurrection of 'Christus Victor' is a decisive triumph over all the powers of evil. It is the new exodus, an act of emancipation from the captivity of sin and death. This mighty act is 'God's way of righting wrong,'[7] of acquitting the guilty sinner, and giving to him the status of a son. Through this work of

---

[1] Prov. 16. 6.   [2] Tobit 12. 9.   [3] Ps. 51. 17.   [4] Ps. 51, 18, 19.
[5] W. T. Davidson, *The Century Bible: Psalms*, I, 265.
[6] Ibid. 266.   [7] Rom. 1. 17. N.E.B.

Christ the enmity is overcome, and fellowship between God and men is restored. Alongside these metaphors of victory, redemption, justification, and reconciliation, the saving deed of God in Christ is also interpreted as a sacrifice. The sacrifices of the old covenant constantly repeated are fulfilled and abrogated 'through the offering of the body of Jesus Christ once for all'.[1] The types and shadows have their ending in the 'full, perfect, and sufficient sacrifice', which they prefigure and interpret. This is the real peace offering, the communion sacrifice, in which the holy life released by death is offered to God and given for the nourishment of men. 'Take; this is my body . . . this is my blood of the covenant, which is poured out for many.'[2] This is the antitype of the peace offering, the covenant sacrifice at Sinai; by his death and resurrection, Christ has established a bond between God and the new Israel, within which his life is received for the increase and sustenance of our strength and welfare. That which the burnt offering prefigured is also fulfilled in him who 'hath loved us, and hath given himself for us an offering and a sacrifice to God for a sweet-smelling savour'.[3] 'The phrase "for a sweet-smelling savour" is used in the Old Testament only of burnt offerings; here it is of course used metaphorically, to express the beauty of a sacrifice that withholds nothing but gives all, even life itself, to God as a tribute of absolute devotion.'[4] In response to this total gift, this complete oblation, Christians are enabled and required to offer themselves as a living sacrifice, holy and acceptable to God.[5] The sacrifice of Christ is also a sin offering. 'For God designed him to be the means of expiating sin by his sacrificial death.'[6] Frequently in the New Testament, the death of Christ is related to sin. Christ died for our sins, he bore our sins in his body on the tree, he offered for all time a single sacrifice for sins, he takes away the sin of the world. Not only the three main types of offering, but what we saw to be the essentials of sacrifice in the old covenant are fulfilled in the sacrifice of Christ. The gift was to be costly and precious; the worshipper was required to offer that which was his own, and was for that reason dear to him. God 'did not spare *his own* Son, but gave him up for us all'.[7] We were bought with a price, with the precious blood of Christ.[8] It

---

[1] Heb. 10. 10.   [2] Mark 14. 22, 24.   [3] Eph. 5. 2. A.V.
[4] F. W. Beare, comment on Eph. 5. 2 in *The Interpreter's Bible*, X, 705.
[5] Rom. 12. 1.   [6] Rom. 3. 25. N.E.B.   [7] Rom. 8. 23.
[8] 1 Cor. 6. 20 and 1 Peter 1. 19.

was not something apart from himself, but his own life that Christ offered. We also saw that in Hebrew thought and practice, sacrifice was both the death of the victim and the offering of its life. We must not equate the sacrifice of Jesus with his death on the cross; his ressurection and ascension, his exaltation and priestly ministry in heaven are the climax of the sacrifice. After slaying the victim, the Aaronic priest entered the sanctuary made with hands that he might offer its life. Having been 'crucified and killed by the hands of lawless men', the great shepherd of the sheep was raised from the dead, and has entered heaven itself with the blood of the eternal covenant.[1] We are saved by the risen Lord who was crucified and ever lives to make intercession for us. 'For if while we were enemies we were reconciled to God by the death of his Son, *much more*, now that we are reconciled shall we be saved *by his life*.'[2] Sacrifice is life offered that life may be received, and this life is in fact received. The sacrifice of Christ is truly effective and fully efficacious because it is the saving deed, the mighty act of God himself. His sacrifice is the supreme sacrament, an instrumental act which initiates or renews communion with God. Finally, Christ's sacrifice fulfils the new insights of the prophets and the psalmists. 'Behold, to obey is better than sacrifice.'[3] For he offered the sacrifice of perfect obedience and perfect love. 'When Christ came into the world, he said, "sacrifices and offerings thou hast not desired . . . lo, I have come to do thy will, O God".'[4] And yet this holy life, this perfect obedience, was consummated in a definite act of sacrifice, in a literal bloody sacrifice. Here is the perfect union of the inner and the outer, of attitude and act, of heart and offering. 'The sacrifice is not one of physical life alone, but neither is it of ethical obedience alone; it is both, in the unity of the Redeemer's personality.'[5] This is the only offering perfect in God's sight – 'the one, true, pure, immortal sacrifice'.[6]

7. Spiritual sacrifices

By his one oblation of himself once offered upon the cross, Christ has made a full, perfect, and sufficient sacrifice for the sins of the whole world.[7] No other sacrifice for sin need be or can be offered. 'It is

---

[1] Heb. 13. 20. [2] Rom. 5. 10. [3] I Sam. 15. 22.
[4] Heb. 10. 5, 7. [5] H. W. Robinson, *Redemption and Revelation*, 254.
[6] W. Bright, in the eucharistic hymn, 'And now, O Father, mindful of the love'.
[7] The Prayer of Consecration, *Book of Common Prayer*.

accomplished.'[1] Christ the Redeemer has made atonement once for all, and believers may 'rest in the finished work' with triumphant assurance. Does this mean that henceforth no sacrifice *of any kind* is to be offered? While strongly affirming 'the scandal of particularity', that at one time, in one place, once for all, Christ offered 'a single sacrifice for sins', the apostles also use sacrificial language to describe the activities of Christians in worship and in service. 'Come to him (the Lord Jesus), to that living stone, rejected by men but in God's sight chosen and precious; and like living stones be yourselves built into a spiritual house, to be a holy priesthood, to offer spiritual sacrifices acceptable to God through Jesus Christ.'[2] The Christian priesthood is to offer spiritual sacrifices; these will be acceptable to God not in themselves, but because they are a response to, and are made possible by, and are offered in union with, the one sacrifice of Christ. They are the outcome, the result, the fruit in cult and conduct of the sacrificial life of the crucified and risen Christ within those who 'come to him'. What are these spiritual sacrifices? From other epistles of the New Testament, as well as from his own, we may infer what the apostle Peter meant by this metaphor. *Praise* and *charity*, thanksgiving offered continually through Christ, and the sharing of our goods for the relief of the needy, are alike spiritual sacrifices acceptable to God.[3] The *gifts* of money sent by the Philippians to Paul in prison are said to be 'a fragrant offering, a sacrifice acceptable and pleasing to God'.[4] Like the sacrifice of a victim on the altar, completed with a drink-offering, the *faith* of the Philippians is a sacrifice, which is likely to be completed by the pouring-out of Paul's life-blood in *martyrdom*.[5] While alive and at work, the apostle Paul is a priest standing at the altar, offering the Gentile converts as a sacrifice. Witness, *evangelism*, missionary work – heaping on his sacred altar the souls he died to save – is a spiritual sacrifice.[6] Finally, offering the body to God as a living sacrifice, *holy living* in all its forms, the consecration of the entire personality, is the true Christian cult, our spiritual worship.[7] From the general contents of his epistle, it is clear that Peter, like Paul, has the whole range of Christian living in mind, in his use of sacrificial language. Following in the steps of the Saviour, bearing unmerited suffering with patience, loving the brethren fervently, doing good to all including the persecutor, maintaining good

---

[1] John 19. 30. N.E.B.   [2] 1 Peter 2. 5.   [3] Heb. 13. 15, 16.
[4] Phil. 4. 18.   [5] Phil. 2. 17.   [6] Rom. 15. 16.   [7] Rom. 12. 1.

conduct among the pagans; all the aspects of the sacrificial life are included. But that does not mean that worship, cultic acts, are excluded. Dr E. G. Selwyn, in his monumental commentary on 1 Peter, calls into question the statement of Hort, and other more recent commentators, that in using the phrase 'spiritual sacrifices', Peter 'cannot be thinking of any ritual acts whatever'. With E. Lohmeyer, he maintains that this section (2. 1–10) 'is packed with pictures and ideas taken from the cultus'. In the context, the spiritual sacrifices are directly related to the cornerstone, Christ crucified and risen, and to the declaration of God's excellencies, his wonderful saving deeds. This atoning work of Christ is certainly proclaimed by the royal priesthood in the new sacrificial way of life, described in the epistle as a whole. But that life is inseparable from worship. 'The "spiritual sacrifices" of which St Peter speaks have been correctly interpreted as consisting in righteousness, self-oblation, deeds of kindness and brotherly love, prayer and praise and penitence. But the background against which our author thought of these sacrifices, and out of which they arose, was the worshipping community, gathered for the celebration of the eucharist.'[1] We misinterpret the apostle, and indeed the Bible as a whole, if, drawing a hard and fast line between worship and service, we then insist that the spiritual sacrifices must belong either to the one sphere or the other. 'The ethics of the Apostolic Church are inseparably bound up with its worship, and the term "sacrifice" is used of the latter as freely as of the former.'[2] Having come to Jesus Christ the living stone, Christians are built into a spiritual house for the holy work of priesthood, for the liturgy of sacrificial worship and service. As was emphasized in chapter I, the two are inseparable aspects of the one whole. It is with one part of this whole that we are here concerned, with the sacrificial worship of the Christian assembly, with the eucharist and its component parts. For it was largely in the doctrine and practice of the eucharist that the biblical conception of worship as offering was both developed and perverted, in the history of the church.

8. The eucharistic sacrifice

'On the Lord's day assemble ye and break bread and celebrate eucharist, having first confessed your sins, that your sacrifice may be pure. Anyone who has a dispute with his fellow is not to come until

[1] E. G. Selwyn, *The First Epistle of St Peter*, 294–7.   [2] Ibid. 296.

they be reconciled, lest your sacrifice be defiled. For it is this which was spoken by the Lord: "In every place and time offer a pure sacrifice unto me, for I am a great King, saith the Lord, and my name is great among the heathen".[1] Whether any of the New Testament eucharistic texts are susceptible of a sacrificial interpretation is open to question, but there can be no possible doubt that from the time of the Didache onwards, the eucharist was regarded as a sacrifice. To this ancient (not medieval) tradition of the church, the writings of the Fathers bear testimony. There are two senses in which most Christians would agree that sacrificial language may rightly be used of the eucharist. It is a sacrifice of praise and thanksgiving. As we commemorate the saving deeds of God in Christ, our hearts are filled with gratitude. This finds expression in the service as a whole, but especially in the Prayer of Thanksgiving offered over the loaf and the cup. While all prayer is to be accompanied 'with thanksgiving',[2] our commemoration of the sacrifice of Christ is in a special sense a *sacrificium laudis*. Furthermore, in response to the mercies of God in Christ, the worshippers offer themselves to God. 'And here we offer and present unto thee, O Lord, ourselves, our souls and bodies, to be a reasonable, holy, and lively sacrifice unto thee.'[3] As in the Old Testament, whole offering, entire gift, oblation, is of the essence of sacrifice. The sacrifice of Christ, once offered, is effective and fruitful in our lives, as through him we offer ourselves in obedience to God. Something more than thanksgiving and self-oblation, however, is implied in the well-known eucharistic hymn of William Bright, a paraphrase and adaptation of the prayer *unde et memores* in the Roman Mass.

> 'And now, O Father, mindful of the love
> That bought us, once for all, on Calvary's tree,
> And having with us him that pleads above,
> We here present, we here spread forth to thee
> That only offering perfect in thine eyes,
> The one true, pure, immortal sacrifice.'

Is this language permissible? In what sense do we 'present' and 'spread forth' to God the one sacrifice of Christ in the eucharist? Both the medieval theologians and the Reformers had an inadequate under-

---

[1] The Didache 14. 2, 3 quoting Mal. 1. 11.   [2] Phil. 4. 6.
[3] *Book of Common Prayer*, the post-communion prayer.

standing of the full biblical meaning of sacrifice. This inevitably prevented them from rightly understanding the relationship between the
one sacrifice of Christ and the eucharist. Under the old covenant, sacrifice was offered for a great variety of reasons, including expiation and
propitiation. Furthermore, the death of the victim was not the end of
the sacrifice, but the necessary means to the release and offering of its
life. Both these truths about sacrifice were largely overlooked both
before and after the Reformation. It was therefore assumed that if the
eucharist was a sacrifice, it must be an expiatory or propitiatory sacrifice
for sin. What Luther called 'the sacrifices of Masses' were offered
largely for this reason. But, as we have seen in the Old Testament, communion and oblation are an essential part of sacrifice. Even more misleading was the simple equation of sacrifice and death. It was assumed
that the sacrifice of Christ was his death upon the cross, and that itself
was regarded too exclusively as an event of the past. Given this misunderstanding, together with the ancient and universal tradition that
the eucharist was a sacrifice, then it followed that the latter must be in
some way a repetition of the sacrifice of Calvary. At the Reformation,
it was rightly seen that this popular view (how far it was taught by
pre-reformation *theologians* is open to question) was contrary to the
teaching of the New Testament. The perfect and sufficient sacrifice of
Christ, offered once for all, need not be and cannot be repeated. Therefore, some concluded, the eucharist is not a sacrifice, but simply the
memorial of a sacrifice. This dilemma (repetition or mere memorial)
was the inevitable outcome of the false assumption, sacrifice is death.
In the light of what the Bible teaches about sacrifice, we must not
identify it *exclusively* with the death of the victim. We must not
separate the act on Calvary from that which preceded it nor from that
which follows it. It was the holy life of the Son of God which was
offered on the cross, and which, having passed through death, is per-
petually effective for the salvation of mankind. The incarnation, the
ministry, the passion and death, the resurrection, the exaltation, the
priestly work in glory – this is the sacrifice of Christ. We preach Christ
as having been crucified. 'The perfect participle marks at once the fact
and the triumph over the fact, its inclusion in the renewed and larger
life of the risen Lord: neither Person nor fact is merely of the past,
they are both of the eternal present.'[1] It is in this sense that we must

---

[1] R. St John Parry, comment on 1 Cor. 1. 23 in Cambridge Greek Testament.

understand the eucharist as the *anamnesis* of the sacrifice of Christ. The
English words 'remembrance' and 'memorial' are both inadequate
translations of *anamnesis*, because they have 'for us a connotation of
something itself *absent*, which is only mentally recollected. But in the
scriptures both of the Old and New Testament, *anamnesis* and the cog-
nate verb have the sense of "re-calling" or "re-presenting" before God
an event in the past, so that it becomes *here and now operative by its effects*.'[1]
The celebration of the Passover was no mere mental recollection of an
event long since past. It was a here-and-now participation in the saving
event commemorated, an event with abiding consequences and pregnant with promise. In the eucharist, Christ is present, and the saving
event is contemporary and operative. For where Christ is present, there
also is his immortal sacrifice. 'If the sacrifice offered once for all is
eternally valid and relevant, and if it is one with Christ who is himself
the sacrifice, then the presence of Christ in the sacrament includes the
effective presence of his sacrifice. It is not a question of recalling something which happened two thousand years ago on Golgotha. The past
is here too the present, as the Lord himself makes the past and eternally
valid sacrifice contemporaneous with us.'[2]   The eucharist is a sacrifice
because *the* sacrifice is present. It is this eternally valid and contemporary
sacrifice that we 'spread forth' in the sacramental signs and tokens.
United by faith with Christ who is present, we are taken up into his
perpetual sacrifice. We do not offer him, but he offers us, the partici-
pants by grace in the effects of his one sacrifice. Like the ancient peace
offering and the burnt offering, the eucharistic sacrifice is communion
and oblation with Christ.

9. Making an offering

Having considered in what way the liturgy as a whole is sacrificial,
we turn now to the component parts. In response to the grace of God
in Christ, declared and mediated through word and sacrament, the
worshippers offer praises, prayers, gifts, and themselves. These are the
spiritual sacrifices to be offered in the assembly. Under the old covenant, song and dance, music and psalm frequently accompanied the
offering of animal sacrifice. Amos associates burnt, cereal, and peace
offerings, with the noise of songs and the melody of harps.[3] Praise was

---

[1] Dom Gregory Dix, *The Shape of the Liturgy*, 161. Italics his.
[2] Gustav Aulen, *Eucharist and Sacrifice*, 192.   [3] Amos 5. 22, 23.

itself part of sacrifice. This was also true of the Graeco–Roman world; hymns were often sung to the deity, especially while the sacrifices were being offered. The Christian psalms, hymns, and spiritual songs were likewise to be sung with thankfulness *to God*.[1] 'Christian hymns are thus themselves the sacrifice so to speak which takes the place of the sacrifice accompanied by the pagan hymn.'[2] Do we not need to recover this objective and sacrificial character of Christian praise? Is our praise in church always in the God-ward direction? Is it offered upwards or offered inwards? Do we not often turn our praise upside down and direct it to ourselves, with the intention of deriving uplift or even pleasant emotions from our 'spiritual exercises'? Certainly song, like music, has an impressive as well as an expressive function; but this should be an indirect consequence, not a deliberate aim. St Augustine defined a hymn as 'a song with praise to God'. When we rise to sing, our primary purpose should be to offer the spiritual sacrifice of praise to God. Like praise, prayer in Israel was closely associated with the offering of sacrifice. Elijah began to pray to God 'at the time of the offering of the oblation', and Daniel 'was speaking and praying . . . at the time of the evening sacrifice'.[3] It was when the sacrifice was offered that 'the people besought the Lord Most High in prayer'.[4] While not abandoning sacrifice, some devout souls realized that the prayers were themselves more important than the offerings they accompanied. 'Let my prayer be counted as incense before thee, and the lifting up of my hands as an evening sacrifice.'[5] The direct outpouring of the heart of the psalmist to God in prayer is itself sacrifice. In the final poem of the suffering servant, offering and intercession are inseparable. He who 'makes himself an offering for sin' also 'made intercession for the transgressors'.[6] Intercession is an essential part of the sacrifice of Christ. In this ministry of intercession, the members of the Body share with the Head. The royal priesthood assembles to represent the human race in the presence of God. 'First of all, then, I urge that supplications, prayers, intercessions, and thanksgivings be made *for all men*.'[7] True prayer is not a didactic exercise, a sermonette addressed to the congregation. It is the offering of the priesthood appointed to represent mankind before God; it is a sacrificial, a costly activity. Together with our

---

[1] Col. 3. 16.
[2] D. G. Delling, *Worship in the New Testament*, 87.
[3] 1 Kings 18. 36 and Dan. 9. 20, 21.   [4] Eccles. 50. 19.
[5] Ps. 141. 2.   [6] Isa. 53. 10, 12.   [7] 1 Tim. 2. 1.

praises and prayers, we offer also our gifts. The ancient sacrifices were costly gifts contributed from the common life. To worship was to 'bring an offering'. The offering in Christian worship is not an interruption, something alien, regrettable, but necessary for the upkeep of the church. There is no need to banish it to the chapel door or hide it away under the cover of a hymn. It is an essential part of our response to God, before whom we are not to appear empty-handed.[1] If it is to be costly, the widespread practice of tipping God with odd coins must be abandoned, and the principles of stewardship and proportionate giving be taken seriously. Within the service, the offertory itself should be impressive, a significant element in the response of the people to the word of God. The collection of the gifts, a necessary preliminary to the offering, may well take place early on in the service, as part of the preparation for worship. The offering itself should follow the ministry of the word and the prayers of intercession. The people should stand for the sentences, procession, and prayer. At the eucharist the bread and the wine should be brought to the table at this point, together with the money gifts. Here we acknowledge that the gifts of creation belong to God and hand them back to him. They represent, however, not only the gifts of God, but also the labour of man; for bread, wine, and money are manufactured. Like righteous Abel, we offer to God in faith and gratitude the products of our toil, that the common life from which they are given may be consecrated to him. The gifts are sacrificial, not only because they are offered to God, but also because they are shared with men. Sacrifice is communion, with God and men. The collection for the needy is *leitourgia* and *koinonia*.[2] Gifts for the support of God's servants and for the furtherance of his gospel are 'a fragrant offering', and sharing our goods with the needy is an acceptable sacrifice.[3] Finally, there is the offering of ourselves. This is not something other than the component parts already mentioned, for in true worship we give ourselves to God *in* praise, prayer, and offering. The bridegroom does not merely give the ring itself to the bride; it is a sign and token of his loyal-love and commitment. In genuine worship, psalms and hymns, prayers and gifts are the signs and tokens of self-oblation. No man has truly worshipped unless he has given himself to God. This sacrifice, this oblation, must be made in life and conduct, in work and service, for the Christian liturgy does not

---

[1] Exod. 23. 15.   [2] 2 Cor. 9. 12. 13.   [3] Phil. 4. 18; Heb. 13. 16.

end with the benediction. In order that it may be made in life as a whole, it should also be made in the context of worship. There should be some place in a church service for such an act of dedication, whether it be in a hymn of consecration, or a prayer of oblation, whether following the sermon or the communion. 'Through the eternal Spirit' Christ 'offered himself without blemish to God.'[1] In union with him and in response to his perfect sacrifice, we are exhorted to offer our bodies as a living sacrifice.

10. Receiving and giving

Worship is offering. This affirmation is often received with nervousness or even alarm. 'The depreciation of the idea of "making an offering" in favour of that of "receiving a blessing",'[2] may be due in part to that radical self-centredness which can and does manifest itself in worship as in all other spheres of life. But it also springs from a commendable concern for the gospel of the grace of God. For in stressing that which man offers in worship, are we not in danger of turning the gospel upside down, and substituting human effort for divine grace? Since the gospel is the good news that God gave and continues to give, should we not assemble to receive? Beyond question! but not to receive without giving. As we saw in the Old Testament, it is a mistake to think of offering and sacrifice simply in terms of man giving to God. Offering is sacrament, sacrifice is 'life offered *in order that life may be received*'. God both gives and takes in the sacrifices of the old covenant, and in that which they prefigure, the sacrifice of Christ, who is both God and man. Both God and men give and receive in sacrifice. For men, the receiving precedes the giving, for all the sacrifices of the People of God follow the act of redemption, the exodus, the cross and resurrection, and are within the covenant of grace. In this context, the offerings of the redeemed are also the sacraments of God, through which his life is mediated and received. They receive the blessings and make the offerings; they also make the offerings and receive the blessings. Distortion takes place when we stress the one and habitually ignore the other. In the biblical sacrifice God takes everything and gives everything. This is to be seen supremely in the sacrifice of the cross. 'Here is a reciprocal and two-way action and attitude in which both giving and taking, both offering and receiving, are united in one

---

[1] Heb. 9. 14.   [2] N. Clark, *Call to Worship*, 12.

single moment of eternity revealed in time. God on the cross gave all, and God on the cross took all. God on the cross offered all, and God on the cross received all. That is the secret of the sacrificial terminology of the atonement.'[1] Christian worship, which is a response to that sacrifice, must exhibit that same reciprocal and two-way relationship. We too are to take all and to give all. Both liturgy and life are distorted if we stress the former exclusively and ignore the latter. The sons of God, grateful, free, and responsible, give as well as receive. 'Graciousness, by definition, cannot "pauperize" the recipient; and *agape* can never be "a charity" in the odious sense of a benefit condescendingly conferred upon a passive beneficiary ... and therefore the divine initiative, the unmerited grace, never relieves us of the responsibility for response; the illimitable riches of God's "grace" and generosity cannot be accepted without the most costly response of which we are capable.'[2] That which God has done and that which man must do, that which God gives and that which man is required to give, must be set side by side.

> 'The sacrifice is offered – Christ himself',
> 'Present your bodies as a living sacrifice.'[3]

---

[1] J. E. Fison, *The Blessing of the Holy Spirit*, 197.
[2] C. F. D. Moule, in *The Parish Communion Today*, 84. (Ed. by D. M. Paton.)
[3] I Cor. 5. 7. N.E.B.; Rom. 12. 1.

Chapter IV

EMBODIED WORSHIP

1. The inward and the outward

'THE whole history of worship might be written round the fascinating and difficult question of the relationship between the outward and the inward.'[1] It is with that relationship that we are concerned in this chapter. Both the outward and the inward are necessarily involved in authentic Christian worship. Why? Because of the nature of God and because of the nature of man. The eternal God whom we worship is revealed and communicated to us through his incarnate Son. 'And the word became flesh and dwelt among us, full of grace and truth.'[2] Our Christian worship derives its distinctive character from the incarnation of the Word of God. We approach the Father through him in whom 'the complete being of the Godhead dwells embodied'.[3] Nor is this incarnate word external to the worshippers, for he is the head of the body, the church. He is the one who includes the many. Christians are in Christ. 'Brought into one body by baptism, in the one Spirit . . . we, many as we are, are one body; for it is one loaf of which we all partake.'[4] It is because we are one body in Christ that we assemble for worship. The congregation of the Lord is the necessary outcome of the incarnation of the word. Prefigured in the history of Israel and in the synagogue assembly, the congregational worship of the church is distinctive and unique.

Embodied worship also answers to the nature of man who is flesh, not pure spirit. 'Thou art man not God, thou art flesh and no angel.'[5] Deeply influenced by Platonism, we tend to think of man as compounded of soul and body, even although we no longer speak of the soul as imprisoned in the body. But 'the Hebrew idea of personality is that of an animated body, not [like the Greek] that of an incarnated soul'.[6] For this reason worship can never, without serious impoverish-

---

[1] C. F. D. Moule, *Worship in the New Testament*, 12.
[2] John 1. 14.   [3] Col. 2. 9. N.E.B.
[4] 1 Cor. 12. 13 and 10. 17. N.E.B.   [5] Thomas a Kempis.
[6] H. Wheeler Robinson, *The Christian Doctrine of Man*, 27.

E

ment, be 'purely spiritual'. Inner devotion requires outward expression;
in words and deeds, in personal and social patterns of activity which
include the body, make use of matter, and are perceptible to the senses.
The human response to the revelation and communication of God in
Christ requires sensible and social embodiment. If the whole personality, 'the body' in the biblical meaning of that phrase, is to be involved
in worship, then the inner devotion of the heart must find adequate
outward expression. The Bible does not set the spiritual over against the
material, and does not relegate and confine worship to the former
sphere. We must be on our guard against an unbiblical dualism, and the
associated tendency to exalt the spiritual and mental and to debase the
sensuous and material. For this can result in the intellectualization and
disembodiment of worship.

The importance of embodied worship may be seen in two directions, psychological and social. The principle taught by psychologists,
that inner attitudes are strengthened and developed by outward bodily
expression, has an important bearing on the devotional life. Indeed, we
can say more than this. For when devotion is absent or dormant, outward performance can often awake or evoke it. We tend to assume that
our actions are always the outcome of our thoughts, emotions, and
volitions. This is only one side of the truth. As the psychologists James
and Lange have emphasized, the expressive actions of the body can also
quicken and strengthen emotion. Action can also evoke emotion.
Anger is increased when a man clenches his fists and strikes a blow. If
he makes himself smile and bursts into laughter, he will probably begin
to feel cheerful. The expressive actions of the body do react for good
or ill on the human spirit. It was the denial of this truth that led Baron
von Hügel to say, 'What a curious psychology which allows me to kiss
my child because I love it, but strictly forbids me to kiss it in order to
love it.'[1] The outward performance of cultic acts, ritual and sacrament,
can evoke devotion when it is dormant or strengthen it when it is
already active. Secondly, not only does the outward evoke and
strengthen the inward, but it also makes it possible for men to act
together. Corporate worship can take place only where there is some
understanding or agreement about what is to be said and done. A
pattern of words is a rite, a pattern of actions a ceremony, and a combination of both a ritual. Corporate worship is possible only where

---

[1] Friedrich von Hügel, *Selected Letters*.

there is ritual. It may be unrecognized, it may be rudimentary, but no group ever worships together without it. Extreme hostility to the outward expression and embodiment, can result in the destruction of communal worship, and the triumph of individualism. This then is the dual value of the cult; it expresses, and by expressing strengthens, the inner devotion, and it enables men to worship together.

In what follows, we shall have in view the three main aspects of outward worship which, taken together, constitute the cult: symbol, ritual, and sacrament. A symbol, which may be a word, a material object, or an action, is that which stands for and represents something else. In the context of worship, that which is represented is often unseen and eternal. A ritual is a pattern of words and actions (rite plus ceremony) – although the term may also be used of a pattern of action unaccompanied by words. A sacrament is the use of outward and visible things to convey an unseen spiritual reality. We shall look at some examples of embodied worship in the Bible and in church history, and then apply these insights and lessons to our contemporary worship.

2. The embodied presence

The embodied worship of ancient Israel may be seen in a familiar Old Testament story.[1] Soon after the capture of Jerusalem and the defeat of the Philistines, David decided to bring the Ark of God into his new capital, a decision dictated by both political wisdom and religious zeal. The solemn procession set out from the house of Abinadab at Kirjath-jearim, with a fitting escort of soldiers for 'the Lord of hosts'. The Ark itself was carried on a new cart, driven by Uzzah and Ahio, the sons of Abinadab. To the accompaniment of an orchestra, David and all the people worshipped the Lord in movement, shout, and song. After the unexpected death of Uzzah, who had presumptuously touched the sacred Ark, David was afraid to take it into Jerusalem, and carried it aside into the house of Obed-edom the Gittite. After a delay of three months, seeing that the Lord had blessed Obed-edom and all his household, David renewed his attempt to bring it into the city. This time, the Ark was carried on the shoulders of men, and when they had advanced six paces, David sacrificed an ox and a fatling. As the procession moved forward, the king, stripped of all his royal robes, wearing only a small strip of cloth (the linen ephod) danced before the Ark

[1] 2 Sam. 6.

of God. His dance was accompanied by the loud shouts of the people
and the incessant blasts of the trumpet. When the Ark had been brought
into the tent prepared for it, David offered burnt offerings and peace
offerings to the Lord. He then blessed and dismissed the people. All
this is very far indeed from being a 'purely spiritual' act of worship.
The Lord of hosts himself is closely associated, if not identified with, the
cultic symbol, the Ark. In Psalm 132, a processional pre-exilic hymn in
which this event is dramatically represented, the Lord is both identified
with and distinguished from the Ark. 'Arise, O Lord, and go to thy
resting place, thou and the ark of thy might . . . let us worship at his
footstool.'[1] We cannot say without qualification that the Lord was
identified with the symbol, but 'there is no doubt that the Ark was
interpreted as the extension or embodiment of the presence of Yahweh,
a counterpart to the divine soul'.[2] The embodied presence could be
seen; the eyes were engaged in the worship. So, too, were the bodies
of the worshippers. This was a solemn procession, a concerted movement, a communal dance. The zeal of David was violently manifested
in physical contortions like those of the whirling dervishes. There was
religious exultation and uninhibited emotion. 'And David and all the
house of Israel were making merry before the Lord with all their
might, with songs and lyres and harps and tambourines and castanets
and cymbals.' With loud shouts and 'the sound of the horn' they all
conspired to make a joyful noise unto the Lord. Procession, dance,
music, and song were consummated in sacrifice and sacrament, in the
total gift of the burnt offering and in the communal feast of the peace
offering. The divine presence and the human response were alike
embodied.

3. Symbol, ritual, and sacrifice

The Ark, the dance, the offering: these features of the story just
narrated may be taken as representing three strands which are woven
together in the Old Testament cult. No hard and fast line can be drawn
between symbol, ritual, and sacrifice, for they merge into one another.
Taken together, they constitute the cult, the embodiment of Hebrew
worship. A symbol is an object taken from the world of sense experi-

[1] Ps. 132. 8, 7.
[2] G. Henton Davies, 'Ark of the Covenant', in *The Interpreter's Dictionary of the Bible*,
I, 222.

ence, to represent the unseen God. The Ark was one of many such cultic symbols. In the second commandment of the decalogue, which in its present form may be dated in the eighth century B.C., the people were forbidden to make or worship before any image of God.[1] In the primitive period, however, as the expression 'to appear before God' suggests, the deity may have been represented in material form. Without condemnation, Hosea mentions pillar, ephod, and teraphim as objects used in the contemporary cult.[2] At the local high place, the presence of God was represented by the stone altar, by the ashera or wooden post, and by the mazzebah or stone pillar. He was sometimes represented as an ox, the symbol of strength and fertility. Whether the ephod and the teraphim were ever at any time images of God is open to question. It is, however, beyond question that in early times his presence and power were associated with concrete objects. The ministry of the prophets and the experience of the exile disentangled the worship of Israel from some of these crude externals. Yet the service of the post-exilic community was not disembodied. The ruined temple was rebuilt and, even although the Ark was now missing from its imageless shrine, a rich profusion of symbols continued to be employed in worship. Employed – for a symbol is not necessarily a static object; it can also, and with greater effect, be an action. At this point symbol and ritual merge.

A ritual is a pattern of action usually, though not invariably, accompanied by words. David danced before the Ark, the symbol of the divine presence. The pattern of action is thus often closely related to the visible representation. The worshippers might stroke the face of, or kiss, the image; bow down before, or dance around, the altar. The Hebrew felt no compunction about using the body in worship. He spread forth or lifted up his hands in prayer. When the solemn procession had moved into the temple courts, the worshippers knelt and prostrated themselves in reverent homage before God. 'O come, let us worship and bow down, let us kneel before the Lord, our Maker!'[3] Another psalmist, away in exile, remembers how he once 'went with the throng, and led them in procession to the house of God, with glad shouts and songs of thanksgiving, a multitude keeping festival'.[4] It is with offering and sacrifice, however, that ritual action is chiefly associated in the Old Testament. Not all offerings were sacrifices. The

[1] Exod. 20. 4–6.　　[2] Hos. 3. 4.　　[3] Ps. 95. 6.　　[4] Ps. 42. 4.

farmer bringing his basket of fruit and setting it down at the foot of
the altar with a confession of faith, was performing a prescribed non-
sacrificial ritual. It was an enacted symbol, a mimetic action, a token
offering sanctifying that from which it was offered – the whole harvest.
The combination of cultic symbol and ritual action, however, comes
to its fullest expression in the offering of sacrifice. Having danced,
David sacrificed burnt offerings and peace offerings before the Ark. In
the offering of sacrifice the inner attitude of the worshipper was expressed, externalized, and embodied. He who felt grateful offered a
sacrifice of thanksgiving, literally. Not that we are to think of sacrifice
simply in terms of man expressing his homage, gratitude, or penitence
in gifts to God. Sacrifices were also sacraments. Through them the
pardon and favour, the succour and grace of God were mediated.
There was a reciprocal activity – homage was given and life was received through the embodied worship. The embodiment is necessary
because man himself is embodied; he belongs to the world of sense and
of spirit.

4. The Christian cult

The transition from the Old to the New Testament is frequently
represented as a progress beyond symbol, ritual, and sacrifice to a
'purely spiritual' worship. The crucial words of our Lord on the subject
of worship, addressed to the woman at the well of Sychar, are frequently misinterpreted in this sense. She is told that the time has
virtually come when the worship of God will no longer be localized on
either Mount Gerizim or Mount Zion. 'The hour is coming, and now
is, when the true worshippers will worship the Father in spirit and
truth, for such the Father seeks to worship him. God is spirit, and those
who worship him must worship in spirit and truth.'[1] This great affirmation must be interpreted from within the Hebrew tradition. Power-
fully influenced by the Hellenistic contrast, material:spiritual, we are
accustomed to think of spirit as the contrary of matter, and to assume
that the spiritual is the immaterial. This is to misinterpret the Bible by
means of an alien philosophy. 'Spirit in the Old Testament is regularly
not an order of being over against matter, but life-giving, creative
activity, and it is in this sense that John commonly uses the word
pneuma.'[2] God, who takes the initiative in seeking men, is creative and

[1] John 4. 23, 24.   [2] C. K. Barrett, *The Gospel According to St John*, 199.

life-giving power. The required response to this living God is worship
'in spirit and truth'. He is to be worshipped in utter sincerity with the
highest element in our personality. He is to be worshipped in accordance with his own real or true nature, now disclosed in Jesus Christ.
Since the true God is disclosed in the word made flesh, the response,
the true worship, can hardly be disembodied. The worship of the new
covenant, a response to the incarnate God, does not reject sign and
symbol, ritual and sacrament. There are two ritual acts, instituted by
the Lord himself at the heart of primitive Christian worship. Baptism
and the Lord's Supper are the enacted symbols, the ritual acts, of the
new covenant. In baptism the *kerygma* was enacted and embodied. And
not only the gospel, but the faith of the candidate, was declared and
embodied in sign and symbol, in ritual act and sacrament. Here also the
outer and the inner, sacramental act and personal confession, 'the washing of water with the word',[1] are one. 'Word and sacrament, *kerygma*
and baptism, stand together to effect and embody initiation into the
household of faith.'[2] This rite of baptism was completed, at least in
some places, by a ritual act of blessing and acceptance, the laying on
of hands. Baptism was initiation into a sacramental fellowship. The
characteristic marks of the primitive church were steadfast continuance
in the apostles' teaching and fellowship, in *the breaking of bread* and the
prayers.[3] While Christian worship was decisively influenced by that of
the Jewish synagogue, the new and distinctive element, the legacy of
the upper room, was the sacred pattern of words and deeds received
from the Lord himself. He had made use of symbols, enacted symbols.
The action with the loaf and with the cup was more than a visual aid,
clarifying and underlining the spoken word; it was an effective symbol.
These ritual acts with the loaf and the cup were instituted to be a joint-
participation in the body and blood of Christ. And so incorporation
and renewal of life in Christ were inseparably associated with the
material (water, bread, wine), with action (washing, eating, drinking),
with symbol, ritual, and sacrament. As contrasted with the elaborate
and complex worship of the temple, the ceremonial acts of the primitive church were elementary and simple. They were performed in an
ordinary place (the open air, the room of a house), by ordinary people,

[1] Eph. 5. 26.
[2] N. Clark in *The Pattern of the Church*, 89. (Ed. by A. Gilmore.)
[3] Acts 2. 42.

wearing ordinary clothes, using ordinary material. This simplicity was not retained. Even within the New Testament, it is possible to trace a growth from the simple to the relatively elaborate. It is in the Apocalypse that we possess the fullest account of this ceremonial worship.[1] As John of Patmos depicts the new Jerusalem by means of imagery taken from the old, so he describes the worship of heaven by means of symbols taken from the liturgy of the church on earth. Here are the bishop's chair, the seats of the elders, the sacred scroll, the liturgical praises and prayers, the sanctus and the amen, the altar and the sacrificial victim. 'The sensible accompaniments of an ordered cultus, music, song, incense, ritual, movements and prostrations, are all there and already taken for granted.'[2] It is impossible to determine to what extent John is drawing upon the symbolism of the Jewish temple, and to what extent he is reflecting the liturgical worship of the churches in Asia Minor at the end of the first century. But there can be little doubt that we have here *some* echoes of early Christian worship. It is not merely verbal. Here word and action, song and movement, mind and body, thought and sense, are combined in the Christian cultus.

5. Elaboration and excess

In the young church the inward and the outward components of worship were present in simplicity and held in balance. With the passage of time, however, the outward element became increasingly prominent, and then predominant. Symbol, ritual, and sacrament were elaborated and given priority, often at the expense of the other component parts of Christian worship. Visual symbols were introduced. Since God had manifested himself in a body, it was inevitable that Christians should seek to represent Jesus Christ, as well as biblical figures and incidents, in artistic form. The earliest Christian art was symbolical. On the walls of the catacombs, Christ is represented by a young shepherd, and by a lamb. Owing, no doubt, to the intensity of the conflict with heathenism, there was, during the first four centuries, a marked restraint in the artistic representation of Christ. There were also protests both against pictures as such and against the growing practice of offering devotion before them, to the one represented in them. The protests and warnings, however, were of no avail, and the pictures 'the books of the unlearned', triumphed. From the fifth century, icons

[1] See especially Rev. 4. 5.   [2] E. Underhill, *Worship*, 92.

became numerous in the east, and survived the ruthless onslaughts of the iconoclastic emperors. An icon is a flat picture, frequently covered with a metal shield for protection. The face and hands of the figure, seen behind the shield, are usually painted in oil on wood. According to the Second Council of Nicaea (A.D. 787), the worship of honour (*timetike proskunesis*) may be offered to the reality represented in the icon, but not the true adoration (*alethine latreia*) which belongs to God alone. 'For honour paid to the image passes over to its original, and he who venerates the image venerates the person depicted in it.' According to Sergius Bulgakov, a consecrated icon is more than a symbol; it is a sacrament. 'The veneration of the holy icons is based not only on the nature of the subjects themselves which are represented, but also on the faith in that grace-filled presence which the church calls forth by the power of the *sanctification* of the icon. The rite of *blessing* the icon establishes a *link* between the image and its prototype, between what is represented and the representation itself. Thanks to the blessing of the icon of Christ, there comes about a mysterious meeting of the believer with Christ. It is the same with the icons of the Virgin and the saints: their icons prolong their lives here on earth.'[1]

This steadily increasing emphasis on the outward and visible is to be seen not only in the development of the static, but also of the enacted, symbol. From the beginning ceremonial acts, kneeling, prostration, the lifting up of the hands in prayer, the kiss of peace, baptism, the laying on of hands, the breaking of bread, were a component part of Christian worship. Just so long as that worship was domestic, the ceremonial acts were few and simple. Either they were the spontaneous outward expression of inner attitudes (e.g. the kiss of peace), or they were the actions necessarily involved in baptizing and 'doing the eucharist'. But when the assembly was transferred from house to basilica, when domestic became public worship, a rapid development and elaboration of ceremonial took place. 'The eucharist was now being performed in a world where every public act secular or religious had always been invested with a certain amount of ceremony as a matter of course. Christian worship was now a public act, and any different treatment of it was simply not thought of.'[2] Solemn processions, the

---

[1] S. Bulgakov, *L'Orthodoxie*, 196. I owe this and the previous quotation to E. L. Mascall, *Theology and Images*, 43.
[2] Dom Gregory Dix, *The Shape of the Liturgy*, 398.

wearing of vestments, the use of the cross and of various insignia, the burning of candles and of incense, the veneration of pictures and icons, were all gradually introduced into the liturgy or the church building. 'They have all either a utilitarian or secular origin in their liturgical use, and are given a particular Christian meaning only through the inveterate instinct of men to attach symbolic interpretations or at least a ceremonious performance to all public acts which are regularly repeated.'[1] The worship of the church at Rome was, for a long period, concise, austere, and simple; but symbol and ceremony were carried to extravagant excess in the medieval church. 'Indescribable richness characterized the church building and the church service. Winged altars, massive reredoses, rood screens, and choir stalls; paintings on stone, wood, and canvas; fonts, holy water basins, chalices, and ciboriums; reliqueries, altar crosses, crucifixes, croziers, censers, and incense boats crowded the structure.'[2] There was a corresponding elaboration of ritual, needless and meaningless processions and movements, multiplied gestures and bows, crossings and genuflections. The advent of the iconoclast and the reformer was long overdue.

6. The reaction

At the Reformation, there was a necessary and justifiable reaction against this excessive symbolism, ceremonialism, and externalism. At first this reaction was not excessive. Martin Luther took a middle course, rejecting and simplifying, but also desiring to retain all such symbols and ceremonies as were not repugnant to the gospel. External rites he held to be necessary, but an absolute value should not be attached to them, and excess of pomp and splendour should be avoided. 'When Christ himself first instituted this sacrament and held the first mass, there were no patens, no chasuble, no singing, no pageantry, but only thanksgiving to God, and the use of the sacrament . . . although I neither wish nor am able to displace or discard all such additions, still, because such pompous forms are perilous, we must never permit ourselves to be led away by them from the simple institution by Christ and from the right use of the mass.'[3] Unlike Luther, John Calvin *was* determined to 'discard all such additions', and to return, as he supposed,

---

[1] Dom Gregory Dix, *The Shape of the Liturgy*, 430.   [2] L. D. Reed, *Worship*, 312.
[3] *A Treatise on the New Testament That is the Holy Mass*, in the *Works of Martin Luther*, Philadelphia Ed. I, 296.

to 'the simplicity that is in Christ.' He reacted in extreme fashion against the medieval embodiments of worship. Art and beauty, symbol and image, lights and eucharistic vestments, instrumental music and choirs, gestures and ceremonies, were all alike abolished. The word of God was enthroned, and the gospel ordinances stripped of all adornment and action not strictly necessary to their performance. Ulrich Zwingli, however, was the principal opponent of embodied worship. Almost Manichaean in his contrast between the spiritual and the material, he abolished the physical and the sensible, symbol and sacrament (the Lord's Supper was retained as an ordinance, not as a means of grace), and relegated worship to the sphere of the mind. This tendency is found in its extreme form in the worship of the Society of Friends. Here the sacraments of baptism and the Lord's Supper, together with all sensible things and fixed forms, are alike rejected in favour of an inward spiritual worship, under the free movement of the Holy Spirit. Even at this extreme, however, the necessity for meeting together is recognized, and the sacramental principle is readily acknowledged in life as a whole.

It is important to realize that the post-reformation reaction against some or many of the outward embodiments of worship, was the outcome of intense conviction born of bitter experience. Widespread corruption in church worship had made the Reformers and their successors keenly aware of the perils of idolatry. There is in some men a strong tendency to become so centred upon and obsessed with symbols and rituals, objects and actions, that they fail to pass beyond them to the God they are intended to mediate. Such 'abominable idolatry' is the supreme, but not the only danger accompanying all embodied worship. Ritualism (the attachment of exaggerated or even absolute value to the due performance of ceremony) and formalism (the substitution of the outward performance for genuine personal and corporate devotion) are the age-long foes of worship 'in spirit and truth'. On the other hand, while understandable, and perhaps inevitable, this hostility to, or suspicion of, the outward embodiments has itself resulted in the creation of an impoverished, distorted, and unbiblical worship. In some traditions the right use (of symbol, ceremony, and sacrament) has been condemned along with the abuse. Within the reformed (i.e. Calvinist) and the puritan-pietist traditions, there has been a powerful reaction against and marked hostility towards embodied worship. Here, all that is addressed to the understanding is 'in', and all appeal to the senses (other than hearing) is 'out'. But this exclusion of the material and the sensuous, of movement and the body, tends inevitably to reduce worship to the exchange of spoken words, whether addressed by God to the people or by the people to God. This weakness is accentuated when the words spoken, in either direction, are largely from the lips of one man. Addressed largely to the understanding, such worship tends to become verbose, abstract, intellectualistic, merely notional.

The history of the church illustrates the tension between the inward and the outward components of worship, and the tendency of Christians to swing to either of two extremes. Taught by that history, we should no longer condemn right use because of abuse, for there is a right use of symbol, ritual, and sacrament. Indeed, not only right, but necessary, because man is both animated body and social being.

7. Words as symbols

Having looked at these aspects of embodied worship selected from the Bible and church history, we may now consider the true role of these three elements of the cult (symbol, ritual, and sacrament) in our worship today.

A symbol, according to the *New English Dictionary*, is 'something that stands for, represents or denotes something else'. The hammer and sickle is the symbol of communism. In this case two small objects, representing industry and agriculture, stand, by general consent, for a reality other and far greater than themselves. The religious symbol is usually an object selected from man's natural or social environment to represent that which belongs to a higher order of being. It is a representation of an unseen reality. Oliver C. Quick, in his book *The Christian Sacraments*, makes a useful distinction between symbols and instruments. The material objects which man himself constructs divide themselves into two classes. 'Some take their character from what is done with them; and these we will call instruments. Others take their character from what is known by them; and these we will call symbols.' A spade is an instrument, a flag a symbol. This distinction, however, is not absolute, for 'every instrument is also a symbol and every symbol also an instrument'.[1] A violin is an instrument, a musical score a symbol; yet the violin can signify and the score be used to produce

[1] O. C. Quick, *The Christian Sacraments*, 5.

music.[1] Significance and instrumentality often go together. Because this is so, although the distinction can be made, no hard and fast line can be drawn between symbol and sacrament. This is especially true of the greatest of all symbols, the Word; it both reveals and works.

The symbols used in worship may be divided into auditory and visual, those addressed to the ears and to the eyes respectively. Spoken words are symbols addressed to the ears. All human language, and not only that used in worship, is of course symbolic. Here meaning and significance are conveyed by the use of a lower medium, the sound waves produced by the human voice. The description of spoken words as auditory rather than visual symbols, is only true, however, if 'eye' is understood literally. For with 'the eye of the mind' words can be seen, as well as heard. 'The words of Amos, who was among the shepherds of Tekoa, which *he saw* concerning Israel.'[2] His oracles were visions; hearing and seeing were inseparable. While this was true in a special way of the ecstatic visions of the prophets, it should also be true, if in a different way, of the one who speaks the oracles of God in the assembly. That which he has heard he should see, in order that his hearers may also hear and see it. As an eastern proverb puts it: 'He is the eloquent man, who turns his hearers' ears into eyes, and makes them see what he speaks of.' Only when this is done, does the word become an effective symbol. If it is to be done, the language used at worship, like that of the Bible, must be concrete, not abstract. It must be picture language addressed to the imagination, the symbol-forming power within man. Like his Master, the effective preacher will use parable and story, illustration and analogy, image and metaphor – 'the sacrament of the imagination'.[3] When words are spoken in the power of the Holy Spirit, they are instrumental symbols. The oracles of God uttered through the lips of inspired men are dynamic – they both reveal and accomplish. The Spirit of God is embodied in the uttered word, which takes on a life of its own, and being power-laden, accomplishes the divine purpose. The word of the Lord speeds on and triumphs.[4] This is why true preaching may rightly be described as sacramental. Wherever the Spirit of God transforms words into instrumental symbols, there is the sacrament of the word. Of course, even when read or spoken in the context of worship, words can be uninspired. They

[1] O. C. Quick, *The Christian Sacraments*, 6. [2] Amos 1. 1.
[3] T. H. Keir, *The Word in Worship*, 65. [4] 2 Thess. 3. 1.

can lose their vitality and potency, their significance and instrumentality. The sacrament of the pulpit, like that of the table, is made valid and effective only by the unseen operation of 'the Lord and giver of life'. He who believes in and relies upon the Holy Spirit, will never doubt or belittle the significance and potency of the spoken word.

> 'A word is dead
> When it is said,
> Some say.
> I say it just
> Begins to live
> That day.'[1]

8. Symbolic objects

God may enter the heart of the worshipper through the eyes as well as through the ears. Symbols may be material objects, designed and shaped by the art and craft of man, to represent the unseen world. The most important material symbol is the church building itself, which in its design, dignity, simplicity, and beauty should bear eloquent, if silent, testimony to God. 'What is required is not only an authentic building, a work of art representing its own time, but an edifice which suggests religious purpose, which speaks reverently of the stupendous fact of divine intervention in human history.'[2] Like the liturgy, the building should be Christocentric. The interior design and arrangement should symbolize the fact that Christ is in the midst of the household of faith. Since he is represented by his minister, the pastor's chair should be prominent and central. If the pulpit and the table are given equal prominence, they will together symbolize the unity of word and sacrament in Christian worship. It is not a matter of any importance whether the pulpit is or is not placed in the centre. Our concern should be to ensure that both pulpit and table are worthy symbols of the centrality of preaching and sacrament. There should also be a worthy symbol of the other sacrament, baptism. Whether near the entrance or at the centre of the building, the baptistery should always be visible. The Bible should remain on the lectern, and the paten and cup should stand on the table even when the sacrament is not being celebrated. A large

---

[1] E. Dickinson, *Collected Poems*, Part I, 89.
[2] L. D. Reed, *Worship*, 19.

empty cross behind the table, or on the wall facing the congregation, is an eloquent symbol of the risen Lord who was crucified. The symbolism of light, taken over by the church from Jewish domestic worship, has great potency. 'It has certainly been one of the things in the physical environment of man which, from the earliest times we know of, has peculiarly impressed him and been most closely associated with his thoughts of the Divine.'[1] The seven-branched candlestick may symbolize the Holy Spirit and his sevenfold gifts. Stained glass, frescoes, framed pictures, statues, may be used to represent the life, death, and resurrection of our Lord. They can also be used to represent the heroes and saints of the Bible and the church, and thus help to create an awareness of the communion of saints. Such symbols are more than 'visual aids' to intellectual understanding; they work at a deeper level. While of special value to children (of all ages!) they should not be despised by any. It is true that, as media, they are inferior to verbal and to enacted symbols. Yet there is no need to sacrifice art in order to appreciate words and actions. 'The Evangelicals, like the Puritans, exalted the ear-gate at the expense of the eye-gate of the soul.'[2] There is no need to continue this one-sided emphasis. We do not honour God by despising the senses with which he has endowed us. Open eyes, as well as open ears, may be engaged in his worship.

9. Ceremonial

A symbol is not necessarily an object; it may be an action. A wooden cross is a symbol; so also is the breaking of bread. The enacted symbol is more suggestive and powerful than the static. It is natural that the inner response of the worshipper to God should find expression in bodily action. 'The Hebrew verb most commonly translated "to worship" (sh-*h*-h) emphasizes the physical expression appropriate to one who comes into the presence of the holy majesty of God: he bows himself down, prostrates himself.'[3] In reformed churches, the words of the Venite are frequently used as a call to worship. 'O come, let us worship and *bow down*, let us *kneel* before the Lord, our Maker!'[4] In many places, they are presumably given a 'purely spiritual' interpretation, for the worshippers do not bow down or kneel! A total response,

[1] E. Bevan, *Symbolism and Belief*, 125.
[2] H. Davies, *Worship and Theology in England*, 236.
[3] A. S. Herbert, *Worship in Ancient Israel*, 10.   Ps. 95. 6.

however, includes the outer and the inner, the physical as well as the psychical. The appropriate postures for prayer are standing and kneeling. The Lord Jesus stood to pray and assumed that his disciples would do the same.[1] In Gethsemane, on the other hand, he knelt, and this posture was frequently adopted by Christians in the apostolic age, usually in special circumstances of deep emotion or urgent need.[2] Standing is expressive of the dignity and confidence of the sons of God; kneeling, of reverence, humility, and submission. It is a good general rule to stand for praise and to kneel for prayer. In the primitive church the prostration of the body (*proskunesis*) was a sign of respect and submission. It was not necessarily accompanied by prayer.[3] In church worship, bowing to the symbolic object, or to the symbolic person, is an eloquent, if silent, expression of reverence towards God. The hands of the worshipper veiling the face like the wings of the seraphim, or held forth palm to palm as when the soldier made his oath, may give outward expression to adoring love and loyal allegiance. 'The right hand of fellowship' extended to others during or after the service, can be the modern equivalent of that ancient 'sacrament of friendship', the kiss of peace. The minister will use his hands in the spontaneous gestures which accompany preaching; they should also be extended in greeting, spread forth in intercession, uplifted in blessing.

As in the Old Testament, the solemn procession provides an opportunity for 'brother ass the body' to participate in worship. At the beginning of the service, the Bible, carried by an officer of the church should precede the minister appointed to read and expound it. This can be an enacted symbol of the centrality and authority of the word of God in the assembly. The processional hymn, with choir and minister or with children and leaders, is possible in a large church with wide aisles. The offering, the climax of worship as response, should be made with impressive ceremonial. The congregation should stand as the stewards process up the central aisle, and the gifts, heaped together on one large plate, should be lifted up over the holy table while the prayer is said.

It is not possible to discuss here the many ceremonies of the various Christian traditions; our purpose rather is to plead for a balanced com-

---

[1] John 17. 1, and Mark 11. 25.
[2] Mark 14. 35; Acts 7. 60; 20. 36; 21. 5; Eph. 3. 14.
[3] 1 Cor. 14. 25.

bination of rite and ceremony, of that which is said and that which is done. In our Christian worship as a whole, the ceremonial element should be characterized by simplicity, dignity, and clarity. The history of worship clearly shows the twin dangers to be avoided, ceremonial carried to excess versus virtually no ceremonial at all. The heirs of the reformed tradition, anxious to avoid the former Scylla, have sailed right into the latter Charybdis. Where ceremony is excessive and over-elaborate, reformation will aim at simplicity and clarity. Where it is lacking, the deficiency must be supplied. For 'the beauty and effectiveness of an otherwise satisfactory service are often marred by deficiencies in necessary ceremonial quite as much as by over-elaboration'.[1] To abolish ceremony is to excommunicate the body from worship.

10. Sacraments

The third element in embodied worship, the sacraments, we have already been considering in discussing the right use of symbol and ceremony. A sacrament is necessarily both: it is a symbol, an enacted symbol, and yet much more than a symbol. For while a symbol represents, a sacrament conveys. It is true that no hard and fast line can be drawn between symbol and sacrament, for a symbol may be instrumental, may convey the reality it represents, and a sacrament should always represent the reality it conveys. Yet in the case of a sacrament the emphasis falls not upon the picture but upon the act, not upon that which is represented, but upon that which is conveyed. A sacrament is a means of grace, an instrumental symbol, an act of God. In baptism and the eucharist, this act of God is related to the gospel. For God reveals and communicates himself through his word, spoken and visible, uttered and embodied, proclaimed by preacher and by sacrament. To separate either sacrament from the proclamation and acceptance of the gospel, is to pervert it. In baptism and eucharist, the grace of God proclaimed in the gospel, is sealed to those who hear and believe the good news. The action of God in the sacraments is also related to the church, where Christ is present through the Spirit. Embodied worship presupposes the presence and activity of the Body of Christ, the fellowship of the Spirit, the congregation of the Lord. Baptism is not a private or domestic ceremony, but initiation into the Body. The

[1] L. D. Reed, *Worship*, 321.

F

eucharist is not 'my communion' but joint-participation in the sacri-ficed life of Christ. The congregation of the Lord is not an optional extra. The sacraments are on the way to corruption when separated from either the word or the fellowship. The action is also essential. We *do* baptism, we *do* the eucharist. It is through the fellowship doing the things ordained and commanded with the water, and with the bread and wine, that God's action takes place. It is the bread *we break* and the cup of blessing *we bless* which is a joint-participation in the body and blood of Christ. The stress falls upon the action, *the church doing* that which Christ has commanded with the material elements. In the eucharist, there is a fourfold action, taking, thanking, breaking, giving.[1] At the conclusion of the liturgy of the word the loaf and the cup, together with the gifts of the people, are carried in solemn pro-cession to the holy table, and with offertory prayer placed upon it. Every eucharist is a harvest thanksgiving, at which the gifts of God upon which man has laboured are offered to him to become the means of grace. The offertory is followed by the eucharistic prayer, in which blessing God over the loaf and the cup, they are consecrated by thanks-giving to be the communion of the body and blood of Christ. Then comes the third action. Taking the loaf in his hands, and raising it so that it may be seen by all the people, the minister breaks bread. It ought not to be, but it is necessary to plead that the service known to the primitive church as 'the breaking of bread' should include *the action* of breaking bread. The use of manufactured wafers, or of tiny sliced cubes of bread, is to be deplored. The fourth action is the distri-bution and consumption of the elements, the communion, whether by the procession of the people to the holy table or of the servers to the congregation. Together with the appropriate words, it is by the performance of this fourfold action that we, the church, 'do the eucharist'.

With reference to the breaking of the loaf, it has already been suggested that we ought not to be afraid of making full use of the *material* of the sacraments. 'God likes matter; he created it.'[2] Are we Gnostics, Manichaeans, or Christian Scientists? Why, for example, are we so afraid of 'our sister water . . . humble, precious, and clean', that we dare only sprinkle a few drops on the forehead of the candidate for baptism? Can such a rite be described as 'the washing of water with the

---

[1] Mark 14. 22, 23.   [2] C. S. Lewis.

word'?[1] Whether it be by pouring water on the head, or by immersion, let us not be afraid to wash 'with pure water' the bodies of those who are being initiated into the Body of Christ. There can only be a fully embodied worship where the ministers of the church have overcome their prejudice against dealing with matter! If God likes it, there is no valid reason why we should dislike it.

What is the relationship between the symbolic and the instrumental, between representation and conveyance in the sacraments? Are they efficacious as means of grace only in so far as their significance is seen and accepted? If this question is answered in the affirmative, the efficacy of the sacraments is made dependent on the spiritual awareness and receptivity of the one using or receiving them. If, on the other hand, it is maintained that the efficacy of a sacrament in no way depends upon the apprehension of its significance, the door is opened to superstition and magic. The truth is that significance and conveyance, that which man apprehends and that which God gives, must neither be equated nor divorced. They must not be equated 'for our own consciousness can never be the measure of the Holy Spirit's activity'. They must not be divorced, for our own consciousness 'is essential to the highest work of the Holy Spirit'.[2] The sacraments are for those who see and accept that which they signify, and yet also believe that God does 'immeasurably more than all we can ask or conceive'.[3] It is necessary that we come with knowledge and faith, yet the gift of God far surpasses our awareness or receptivity. 'Both instrumentality and significance or expressiveness are fundamental constituents of sacramental being, and neither must be made simply adjectival to the other.'[4]

Now it is because far more is conveyed by the sacraments than can be apprehended by the mind, that the celebration of the eucharist truly complements the preaching of the word. For the spoken word is necessarily addressed to the mind, although through the mind it can also stir the emotions and move the will. Worship which relies too exclusively on the spoken word, is always in danger of becoming abstract, notional, intellectualistic. As enacted symbol, as 'visible word', the sacrament too is addressed to the mind; but it is far more than a visual aid to a fuller understanding. Indeed, the mind of the worshipper may

[1] Eph. 5. 26.
[2] H. Wheeler Robinson, *The Christian Experience of the Holy Spirit*, 187.
[3] Eph. 3. 20. N.E.B.
[4] O. C. Quick, *The Christian Sacraments*, 220.

here cease to enquire, because he is aware of the presence of inexpressible mystery. Such an awareness is 'the deepest and most fundamental element in all strong and sincerely felt religious emotion'.[1] Here God gives not only to the surface mind and to the mind in depth, but to the whole personality, the body, including the physical which is involved in seeing, tasting, eating, drinking. 'The body of our Lord Jesus Christ . . . the blood of our Lord Jesus Christ . . . preserve *thy body and soul* unto everlasting life.'[2] In these various ways, the sacrament complements the word. Only when the one comes to its climax in the other is the worshipper offered a full diet. In the celebration of the eucharist, with the reading and preaching of the word, the whole personality of the believer is involved in worship and nourished by God.

11. Total worship

On one occasion the Lord Jesus Christ was asked which of the six hundred and thirteen commandments of the Law of Moses came first in importance. He replied, 'The Lord our God, the Lord is one; and you shall love the Lord your God with all your heart, and with all your soul, and with all your mind, and with all your strength.'[3] Misguided attempts have sometimes been made to give exact definitions of these words, heart, soul, mind, and strength. But they are the words of a poet, not of a psychologist; they are rhetorical, not scientific. In the Shema, man is required to love God *with his whole being*. Every facet of his many-sided life, every faculty of his personality, is to be involved and engaged in that worship and service which is God's due. The great commandment, which of course applies to life in general, is true of the cult in particular. Thought and emotion, volition and action, mind and body, the whole man, is to be involved in acknowledging the supreme worth of God.

There cannot be a total act of worship if certain aspects of the whole personality of man are excluded, or at least inadequately expressed. A tradition of worship predominantly verbal, notional, intellectual, must be so reformed that the sentiments and the senses, movement and action, matter and the body, are also included and involved. Our task

[1] R. Otto, *The Idea of the Holy*, 26.
[2] *Book of Common Prayer*, The Communion Service.
[3] Mark 12. 29, 30.

is to overcome the false antithesis between the spiritual and the material, the soul and the body, the inward and the outward, and recover biblical wholeness.

> Let us not always say
> "Spite of this flesh today
> I strove, made head, gained ground upon the whole!"
> As the bird wings and sings,
> Let us cry "All good things
> Are ours, nor soul helps flesh more, now,
> Than flesh helps soul." [1]

[1] Robert Browning, *Rabbi ben Ezra.*

Chapter V

LIBERTY AND LITURGY

1. The twin pillars

JACHIN and Boaz – such were the names given to the twin pillars of bronze, twenty feet in circumference and thirty feet high, which stood on each side of the entrance to Solomon's temple.[1] They were symbolic objects, the significance of which is not known with any degree of certainty. If, like the apostle Peter, we describe the new temple, the Christian church, in terms of the old, we may speak of liberty and liturgy as the twin pillars which together symbolize two essential elements in the worship of God. 'What Christ has done is to set us free'.[2] That glorious liberty of the sons of God will find expression in worship as in life. 'For we are the true circumcision who worship by the Spirit of God and glory in Christ Jesus.'[3] The worship of the new covenant is inspired by the Holy Spirit, and 'where the Spirit of the Lord is, there is freedom'.[4] Yet this same Spirit who is manifested in the 'inspired spontaneity' of the assembly, is also the one source of true order in the redeemed fellowship, as in creation and society. He requires that 'all things should be done decently and in order'.[5] Liturgy has to do with order. It is the work, the worship-service of the people of God, *ordered* so as, on the one hand, to declare the whole gospel, and, on the other. to enable the congregation to make an adequate response. It is in this sense that the word 'liturgy' is used through this chapter.

The contrast between these two complementary elements in worship may be drawn out in a variety of ways. It is to be seen in the tension between freedom and tradition, spontaneity and order, the extempore and the liturgical, the charismatic and the formal, the prophetic and the sacramental. Some of these antitheses can be misleading, but they are useful in drawing attention to contrasted types of worship familiar to us in the Bible, in history, and in contemporary church life. Not that either is ever entirely absent. For even in a tradition where one of the two elements has become predominant, the other is also represented.

---

[1] 1 Kings 7. 21. [2] Gal. 5. 1. N.E.B. margin. [3] Phil. 3. 3 margin.
[4] 2 Cor. 3. 17. [5] 1 Cor. 14. 40.

In the Mass of the Roman Catholic Church, there is a stereotyped pattern of word and action; here fixity and form, the traditional and the liturgical, the priestly and the sacramental, are at a maximum. Yet even in the Mass, epistle and gospel, collect and 'proper' change and vary, and there is room for freedom and spontaneity in preaching. In the Quaker Meeting, on the other hand, freedom, informality and spontaneity are predominant. Yet even here there is the fixed time and place of meeting, the recognized procedure, the traditional contributions of extempore prayer and spoken ministry. Liberty and liturgy are both present, even where the first is distrusted or the second unacknowledged. The twin pillars, however, may differ greatly in size. In the history of the church, liturgy was developed at the expense of liberty, and in reaction liberty was recovered at the expense of liturgy. What then is the ideal relationship between them? To what extent should worship be ordered and to what extent should it be free? This is an important issue between the divided churches, especially those of our own country. Free Churchmen reject the Book of Common Prayer not, for the most part, because they object to the contents, but because they believe such a degree of fixity seriously restricts the freedom of the Holy Spirit. Anglicans criticize Free Church worship not because they disagree with freedom in principle, but because such a degree of liberty results in disorder and fails to provide an adequate and worthy medium for common prayer and praise. Can the positive elements in these two positions, for so long regarded as contradictories, be combined in a new creative synthesis? What would be the nature of our worship if both liberty and liturgy were valued equally? We shall look at these two elements in the worship of the Bible and of the church, and then consider how they may be combined in our worship today.

2. Actions not words prescribed

It is possible to select from the worship of Israel extreme examples of unrestrained liberty and of prescribed liturgy. The frenzied songs and utterances of the professional prophets 'coming down from the high place with harp, tambourine, flute, and lyre before them' are entirely uninhibited and spontaneous. They are attributed to the direct inspiration of the Spirit of the Lord.[1] At the other extreme is the liturgy

[1] I Sam. 10. 5, 6.

prescribed for the presentation of the first-fruits.[1] Here the Israelite is told not only what he is to do, but also what he is to say as he does it. The liturgy, which is both a confession of faith and a prayer of thanksgiving, interprets the offering of the basket of produce. These examples, however, are extremes. Speaking of the Old Testament as a whole, it would be true to say that directions are given for that which is to be done, rather than for that which is to be said in worship. The worshipper was required to follow the customary or commanded pattern of action, but was free to choose the words of praise or prayer which accompanied the action. Leviticus, for example, is a collection of rubrics; it is predominantly concerned with what is to be done and how it is to be done. There is little or no interpretation of the ritual acts, nor is the worshipper told what to say. It is not a book of rites but a book of ceremonies. Not that the *communal* offerings were made in silence, or were accompanied only by the praises and prayers of individuals. It was H. Wheeler Robinson who first taught us to study Leviticus and the Psalter together; in the former we have the actions, in the latter some of the words accompanying the actions. It is now generally accepted that many of the psalms had a cultic origin, or at least were adapted to the worship of the temple. Created and collected by the priests and cultic prophets, many of these sacred songs and prayers were chanted by the temple choir at the great national festivals or while the sacrifices were being offered. Psalm 135, for example, is a liturgical hymn, sung antiphonally by solo voices, temple choirs, and congregation, probably at a festival. At the conclusion the laymen, the priests, the Levites, the temple servants, praise God in turn and then in chorus.

> 'O house of Israel, bless the Lord!
> O house of Aaron, bless the Lord!
> O house of Levi, bless the Lord!
> You that fear the Lord, bless the Lord!
> Blessed be the Lord from Zion,
>   he who dwells in Jerusalem!
> Praise the Lord!'[2]

On other occasions, the music and the chanting were the background against which the worshippers offered their own individual prayers. It

---

[1] Deut. 26. 1–11.   [2] Ps. 135. 19–21.

was when the sons of Aaron sounded the trumpets and made a great noise to be heard, and the singers praised him with their voices in sweet and full-toned melody, that the people besought the Lord Most High in prayer.[1] Sometimes the people prayed the liturgy itself, at other times they offered their own prayers during the liturgy. In the case of a domestic sacrifice, while that which was to be done was prescribed, there was ample room for extempore prayer. It was while Elkanah and his family worshipped and sacrificed to the Lord at the annual festival at Shiloh, that Hannah, deeply distressed, prayed to the Lord. The simple communion sacrifice was the occasion for intense personal prayer.[2] To sum up, the Israelite, whether worshipping alone or with others, did sometimes use liturgical as well as extempore praises and prayers. But custom and law alike were concerned far more with prescribed actions than with prescribed words. In the sphere of worship there must be order in what you do, although there may be liberty in what you say as you do it. Here we have a principle of permanent validity for the ordering of the worship of the People of God.

3. Synagogue worship

In the non-sacrificial worship of the Jewish synagogue the two elements, freedom and order, were finely blended. While the temple stood, the synagogue was primarily a school of instruction rather than a house of prayer. It was a continuation of the assembly under Ezra the scribe when 'they read from the book, from the law of God, with interpretation; and they gave the sense, so that the people understood the reading'.[3] We know from the gospels that in the synagogue service in our Lord's time there were readings from the law and the prophets, and, if a suitable or gifted speaker was present, a message or exposition of the scriptures. More detailed information about the liturgy of the synagogue can be obtained from the Mishna. Although produced about A.D. 200, it is a compilation of older material. While allowance must be made for the rabbinical habit of attributing later material to former generations, yet there can be little doubt that 'the Mishna contains fairly reliable accounts of Jewish practices that prevailed during New Testament times'.[4]

It is probable that there were benedictions both before and after the

---

[1] Eccles. 50. 16–19.   [2] 1 Sam. 1. 1–18.   [3] Neh. 8. 8 margin.
[4] A. Cronbach, 'Jewish Worship', in *The Interpreter's Dictionary of the Bible*, IV, 895.

reading of the law and the prophets in our Lord's time. The recitation of the Shema, the creed of Judaism, ('Hear, O Israel: the Lord our God is one Lord' etc.) and the prayers known as the *Eighteen Benedictions* were added later. Paul P. Levertoff gives the following outline of 'the normal synagogue service on a Sabbath morning at least after the year A.D. 70'.[1] The 'ruler' would summon 'the minister' to invite a member of the congregation to recite the Shema and the three benedictions connected with it. To his bidding, 'Bless ye the Lord, the Blessed One', the congregation responded, 'Blessed be the Lord, the Blessed One, for ever and ever.' The leader then recited the *Yotzer* and the *Ahabah*, the two benedictions or prayers which preceded the Shema. After the confession of faith, the Shema, had been recited antiphonally, the leader concluded with the third benediction. The 'minister' then called upon another layman to lead the group of prayers known as the *Shemone 'Esreh*, or *Eighteen Benedictions*, which on a Sabbath were reduced to seven. For these the congregation stood, and the leader recited them on the platform facing the ark. To each, the congregation responded with *Amen*. This liturgy of confession and prayer was followed by a reading from the law, the whole of which was read through in three years. A translator stood by the reader and rendered the Hebrew into Aramaic a verse at a time. This was followed by a lesson from the prophets, the choice of which was left to the reader and which was translated three verses at a time. Both readings were preceded and followed by appropriate benedictions. If a suitable person was present, the readings would be followed by a sermon, for which the preacher sat. It is likely, but by no means certain, that psalms were also said or chanted. Within this prescribed order there was ample room for liberty of utterance. Any member of the congregation could be invited to lead the prayers or to address the people. 'After the reading of the law and the prophets, the rulers of the synagogue sent to them, saying, "Brethren, if you have any word of exhortation for the people, say it." '[2] Such an invitation might be extended to gifted laymen. Furthermore, although certain prayers were customary and prescribed, the actual content and wording of the prayers was not fixed, and varied considerably from place to place. 'There was always an aversion among the Rabbis to making prayer a matter of fixed formulas. Some Rabbis,

[1] *Liturgy and Worship*, ed. by W. K. Lowther Clarke, 76, 77.
[2] Acts 13. 15.

for instance, held that one should include something new in one's prayer every day. (Ber. 29b); and even in the third century A.D. much latitude prevailed as regards personal deviations in phraseology.'[1] No doubt there was frequently 'something new' in the Sabbath prayers of the synagogue, arising out of the common life, the contemporary situation, the immediate circumstances. The 'messenger of the congregation' could extemporize within a given framework. Here then is the extempore and the liturgical, the novel and the traditional. The twin pillars of freedom and order stood before 'the little sanctuary'.

4. The spirit of Jesus

Freedom was one of the outstanding characteristics of the spirit of Jesus. To his contemporaries he was not a traditionalist, but a revolutionary, and as such he was crucified. He refused to put the new wine into the old skins. The new life, the new spirit, the new movement, could not be confined within the old forms of Judaism.[2] He rejected not only 'the tradition of the elders', but also the distinction between clean and unclean which was part of the written law.[3] He foretold that the existing temple would be destroyed, and in some sense, rebuilt.[4] When asked why his disciples did not fast, Jesus enunciated a principle of far-reaching importance. He rejected the practice of the Pharisees of fasting at stated times according to prescription. There are times, such as a wedding, when fasting is out of place. A religious act should fit the occasion, be appropriate in the circumstances.[5] Did Jesus apply this principle to prayer as well as to fasting? Did he start from 'the other end in teaching the discipline of prayer – not from *chronos*, time set by the clock, but from *kairos*, waiting for the moment that drives us to our knees'.[6] We may certainly deduce from the evidence supplied by the gospels of Mark and Luke that Jesus resorted to prayer at the appropriate times – in moments of crisis, decision, need, or exaltation. We simply do not know whether he himself had regular daily habits of prayer, or taught such a rule to his disciples. It is unlikely that the Lord's Prayer was given originally as a set prayer to be said; it was rather intended as a general guide and pattern for all prayer.[7] Nor is it likely that Jesus himself used 'set prayers' in personal converse with God.

[1] P. P. Levertoff, op. cit., 73. [2] Mark 2. 18–22.
[3] Mark 7. 1–23. [4] Mark 14. 58 and 15. 24. [5] Mark 2. 18–20.
[6] J. A. T. Robinson, *Honest to God*, 103.
[7] Matt. 6. 9; but contrast Luke 11. 2.

The little evidence there is indicates that he probably used extempore prayer, appropriate to the occasion.[1] He conversed with the Father face to face, with the freedom and intimacy appropriate to his unique filial relationship. This fact has an important bearing upon the nature of Christian prayer and worship, for the Spirit which rested upon Jesus has been given to all believers, making them sons of God by adoption and grace. 'God has sent the Spirit of his Son into our hearts, crying "Abba! Father!" '[2] The Holy Spirit poured out upon the church on the day of Pentecost, and bestowed upon all those subsequently baptized into the one body, leads all believers into a relationship with God characterized by trust and love, intimacy and freedom. The Spirit, who reproduces in believers 'the mind that was in Christ Jesus', is the Spirit of sonship and liberty. And it was in the church assembled for worship that Christians experienced most fully 'the glorious liberty of the sons of God'. In 1 Corinthians 14 we have a description of this charismatic, pentecostal worship. In this assembly the movement and inspiration of the Holy Spirit is unfettered, and all the members are free to contribute according to their gifts. Here there is direct revelation, filial intimacy, ecstatic utterance, inspired spontaneity, enthusiastic participation, sovereign freedom. If there was a pattern, a recognized sequence, it is not discernible. While seeking to rectify the disorder, the apostle makes no attempt to prescribe or enforce any particular 'order of service'. Here there is a minimum of order and a maximum of freedom. 'Christ set us free to be free men.'[3] Applied in the context to the Mosaic Law, these words had a wider application. In accordance with the Spirit which rested upon Jesus and was now shared by his disciples, there was a flexibility of approach, an unmistakable tendency to exalt spontaneity and freedom above inflexible rule and prescribed form.

5. Tradition and pattern

We must not, however, overdraw the contrast between freedom and order, spontaneity and pattern in the apostolic age. For the worship of the early Christians was rooted and grounded in a dual tradition, that of the Jewish synagogue and of the upper room. The Lord Jesus himself had worshipped habitually in the synagogue,[4] and had

---

[1] Matt. 11. 25, 26.   [2] Gal. 4. 6.   [3] Gal. 5. 1. N.E.B.
[4] Luke 4. 16.

no doubt often been invited to lead the prayers as well as to read and expound the scriptures. His disciples continued to worship in the synagogues until they were expelled. The first churches were entirely Jewish, and inevitably they continued to use the customary forms of Jewish synagogue worship, the readings, the teaching-exposition of scripture, prayer, and praise. We cannot, of course, assume that the worship of a predominantly Gentile church would have been so decisively influenced by the pattern and traditions of Jewish synagogue worship. There is, for example, little indication that the worship of the church at Corinth owed much to the synagogue. On the other hand, Justin Martyr refers to the reading of the scriptures and to preaching as an established part of the worship of *Gentile* churches in the middle of the second century.[1] The degree of Jewish influence on Christian worship may have varied considerably from place to place; but it has been decisive and enduring. And, as we have seen, the synagogue service had order and pattern, and both free and liturgical prayer.

The other, and distinctively Christian source of our worship is the upper room. There, on the night of his betrayal, our Lord gave to his disciples that sacred *pattern* of words and deeds by which they were to commemorate his death, enter into communion with him, the risen Lord, and anticipate his advent in glory. This pattern of words and deeds was 'traditioned', handed down in the church, and *regarded as authoritative for procedure*. Thus Paul corrects the disorders in the celebration of the Lord's Supper by reminding the Corinthians of that which he had received from the Lord and delivered to them.[2] They were to repeat the sacred acts and words according to the pattern given in the upper room. This dual tradition, derived from the synagogue and the upper room, was the framework, the ground pattern for Christian worship. It contributed the element of order within which the worshippers were free. These two influences were present from the beginning. There are also other scanty indications within the New Testament of the use of fixed forms, of hymns and psalms, of creeds and doxologies, of exclamations and responses. In the *Apocalypse*, written towards the end of the first century, we can learn something of the contemporary worship of the churches. While the outbursts of praise and prayer are ecstatic and spontaneous, they are also unanimous and ordered.

[1] *Apology*, 1. 67.   [2] 1 Cor. 11. 23-26.

Here already is music and song, ritual movement and liturgical prayer.

To sum up, in the New Testament as a whole freedom and tradition, spontaneity and order are both present, and implicitly accepted as complementary. In the sentence with which Paul concludes his discussion of the worship of the Corinthian church, both elements alike are extolled. The suppression of inspired spontaneity and the acceptance of chaotic disorder are alike proscribed. 'In short, my friends, be eager to prophesy; do not forbid ecstatic utterance; but let all be done decently and in order.'[1]

6. Liberty in fetters

During her long and chequered pilgrimage down the centuries, the church was unable to maintain the creative and fruitful relationship between freedom and pattern in worship, characteristic of the apostolic age. In spite of the vigorous protest of Montanism and other attempts to revive charismatic worship, there was an increasing tendency to develop liturgy at the expense of liberty. The presence of enemies without and heretics within made it necessary for the church to safeguard her faith and strengthen her unity. The same factors which led to the formation of the canon of apostolic writings, to the formulation of the creeds and to the establishment of an official ministry, also encouraged the development of liturgical forms of worship. Indeed, the common liturgy, including as it did scripture, preaching, and sacrament, was itself the most powerful apologist of the faith and bond of unity. The traditions and forms of worship received from synagogue and upper room provided the church with a recognized sequence, and a settled and orderly pattern of action. As in the Old Testament, it was a pattern of action rather than a pattern of words, which was prescribed by custom. While certain words and formulas were used habitually in Christian worship from the apostolic age onwards, most of the words used in the service were not formulated, and certainly not fixed.

It is true that in the Didache (*c.* A.D. 120) written prayers of thanksgiving are provided as a guide ('give ye thanks thus') for presbyters celebrating the eucharist. But they are followed by the instruction

---

[1] I Cor. 14. 39, 40. N.E.B.

'permit the prophets to offer thanksgiving as much as they desire'.[1] Evidently the need for common order was recognized, but such prayers were still regarded as inferior to the extempore thanksgivings of the inspired prophets. In the *First Apology* of Justin Martyr, written about A.D. 150, we have the earliest full account, outside the New Testament, of the Christian service. There is an orderly sequence of *action:* lections, sermon, intercession, offertory, thanksgiving, distribution and communion, almsgiving. But the *words* of the eucharistic prayer, and presumably also of the intercessions, are not formulated and fixed. For 'the president offers prayers and thanksgiving *according to his ability*, and the people respond with the Amen'.[2] Such language could hardly be used of a prayer read from a manuscript or memorized, and must be taken to imply that the eucharistic prayer, even if it followed a customary pattern and contained traditional material, was extempore.

In the *Apostolic Tradition* of Hippolytus (*c*. A.D. 215) the bishop is still permitted to extemporize the eucharistic prayer. There is a common pattern, but not a fixed form of words. 'It is not altogether necessary for him to recite the same words which we said before, as if learning to say them by heart in his thanksgiving to God; but according to the ability of each one he is to pray.' The bishop is free to use the set form or to offer extempore prayer. 'The evidence, therefore, is complete and definite, that in Rome in the second and third centuries, and in the eastern churches also, the gift of extempore prayer was greatly valued, and was allowed to be exercised by competent persons even in the eucharistic canon, although even at this early period written liturgies (of a somewhat meagre type) already existed.'[3] Unfortunately, this evaluation of extempore prayer was lost in the course of time. 'When later the *Apostolic Tradition* was translated into Arabic and Ethiopic, the notion of fixity and uniformity had come in and the words "there is absolutely no necessity" were changed to "it is absolutely necessary"!'[4] The tendency to formulate and fix the words of the prayers proved to be stronger than the love of liberty in worship.

---

[1] Didache 10. Some scholars, however, believe that these prayers were intended for the agape, not the eucharist.

[2] *Apology*, 57.

[3] I have taken this and the previous quotation from the essay, 'Extempore Prayer', by C. Harris in *Liturgy and Worship*, ed. by W. K. Lowther Clarke, 766, 767.

[4] T. S. Garrett, *Christian Worship*, 53.

7. Variable elements

If liberty was restricted, variety was still maintained in church worship, when the words of the great liturgies were formulated. For there were various ways in which spontaneity and freedom, variety and flexibility could be maintained and expressed. The eucharistic rite comprises the *ordinarium*, the *proprium*, and the free elements.[1] 'The ordinary' is that part of the rite which remains constant throughout the church's year; it is the unchanging basis, the framework of the liturgy. 'The propers' are those parts of the rite which vary with the Christian year, whether with the temporal (the commemoration of the saving deeds of God in Christ) or the sanctoral (the commemoration of the saints) cycle. In this respect, there was much less variety in the eastern rites. 'The Eastern choice of variable prayers is limited to a much smaller number of *sets* of prayers than are found in the Western rites, though variation goes further in that when the prayers do vary, they *all* vary.'[2] In the Western rites, chants, epistles, gospels, collects, prefaces vary from season to season, or from Sunday to Sunday. In this connection the Gallican and Mozarabic rites are of special interest. 'The outstanding peculiarity of these rites is their treatment of the eucharistic prayer, in which, except for the text of the sanctus and the paragraph containing the narrative of the institution, the whole eucharistic prayer is varied, or "proper", on every liturgical occasion.'[3] By means of these various 'propers', the liturgy was adapted to the changing seasons, made relevant to the commemoration, in sequence, of the saving acts of God. It must also be remembered that in addition to 'the ordinary' and 'the propers' there was some place for a free element, not prescribed either permanently or by season. In 'the biddings' which followed or preceded the sermon (if any) the priest was free to invite the people to pray for the living and the dead, or to offer such prayers himself. Most of all, where the preaching of the word itself survived, the charismatic, prophetic element could find expression. For the words of the preacher were not fixed. But with all these necessary qualifications, it can hardly be denied that in the post-Constantinian church the liberty of the Spirit was 'cabin'd, cribb'd and confin'd'. If liberty had not

[1] W. Hahn, *Worship and Congregation*, 56.
[2] Dom Gregory Dix, *The Shape of the Liturgy*, 530.
[3] Ibid., 551.

been expelled from the worship of the church, she was everywhere in fetters, awaiting the day of deliverance.

8. Liturgy reformed

The Reformation has often been represented as a widespread resurgence of liberty; the reaffirmation of the freedom of the Christian man, as against the tyranny of the medieval church. This popular notion is all the more misleading, for the element of truth it contains. In fact, the original reformers did not accept the principle of toleration, or recognize freedom of conscience in matters of belief or in forms of worship. In spite of this, however, the Reformation from the beginning resulted in a limited restoration of liberty in church worship. The use of the vernacular, the central place given to the preaching of the word, the endeavour to return to primitive simplicity, all contributed in different ways to the restoration of freedom. As a result of the work and influence of Luther and Calvin, this enlargement of the sphere of liberty in worship resulted not in the rejection, but in the reform of liturgy. There was no return to pentecostal or charismatic worship. Luther did not discard, but drastically reformed the eucharistic liturgy, and by his translation of the scriptures and composition of hymns and prayers, made a notable contribution to the enrichment of worship. The joy, assurance, and freedom of the Christian man returned with the evangelical doctrine of justification by faith. Gospel preaching, congregational hymn-singing, and common prayer were joined together. The new liberty moved within the new liturgy.

While Calvin was a more radical reformer of worship than Luther, he too recognized the importance, indeed the necessity, of set forms of worship. 'Concerning a form of prayer and ecclesiastical rites, I highly approve of it that there should be a certain form from which ministers be not allowed to vary. That first, some provision be made to help the unskilfulness and simplicity of some; secondly, that the consent and harmony of the churches one with another may appear; and lastly, that the capricious giddiness and levity of such as effect innovations may be prevented . . . therefore, there ought to be a stated form of prayer and administration of the sacraments.'[1] Common order is necessary because there are misguided and ungifted ministers (!), as a bond of unity, and as a curb to individualism. 'At the same time, it

[1] Op. XIII, 70, quoted by W. D. Maxwell in *Ways of Worship*, 121.

was recognized from the beginning, in the reformed churches, that opportunity ought to be given for free or extemporaneous prayer to express the mood and needs of the moment and to give liberty to the impulsion of the Holy Spirit.[1] It was not, however, this recognition of the value of free prayer, but Calvin's approval of a 'form from which ministers be not allowed to vary', which was decisive for the worship of the reformed churches in the immediate post-Reformation era. With the exception of sermon, lessons, and psalms, 'everything else, including the confession and the prayers before and after the sermon, was read from the same text Sunday after Sunday'.[2] In this respect, there was even less variety than before the Reformation.

9. Liturgy enforced and rejected

In our own country, the creative genius of Archbishop Cranmer combined what was of value in the old rites with the new insights and positive gains of the Reformation. The Book of Common Prayer was a magnificent achievement. The clarity and dignity of its style, the orderly arrangement of the services, the provision for both Sunday and daily worship, the extensive use of the scriptures, the encouragement of lay participation, the biblical content of the praises and the prayers, are among its virtues and merits. Yet it was an intolerable restraint to liberty in worship in two different ways. No provision was made within it for either free or extempore prayer. Furthermore, the Anglican liturgy, unlike those of the Lutheran and Calvinist churches, was not permissive, but obligatory. For this fixed liturgy was now by an enactment of the state imposed upon all the citizens of the realm. This particular way of restraining liberty was something new in the history of the church, which in former ages had neither desired nor attempted complete uniformity in worship. There had always been a certain amount of local diversity and freedom, even in the medieval church. This attempt by the secular government to enforce uniformity was destined to bedevil the development of worship in this country for over three centuries. For in resisting an imposed uniformity, some Christians and churches were almost inevitably driven into opposition to liturgy as such. The persecuted may be forgiven for failing to distinguish between things that differ, between liturgy and an inflexible

---

[1] Op. XIII. 70, quoted by W. D. Maxwell in *Ways of Worship*, 121.
[2] H. G. Hageman, *Pulpit and Table*, 37.

state-enforced liturgy. For a time, however, some Christians were able to make this distinction. It has often been pointed out that in rejecting the Book of Common Prayer, the Puritans were not rejecting liturgy as such. 'The moderate Puritans were not opposed to a liturgy in principle but only to a particular liturgy, the Book of Common Prayer; they objected, not to liturgical forms as such, but to the "stinted forms" of the Prayer Book.'[1] Prescribed forms of prayer were valued, provided they did not exclude extempore prayer, upon which they tended to set a higher value. But almost inevitably in process of time, objection to the contents of a particular liturgy and (what is not the same thing) objection to the enforcement of a particular liturgy, became objection to all liturgy as such.

It would, however, be an over-simplification to put this forward as the main reason why the nonconformists in this country rejected the Anglican liturgy. The extreme left wing of the Reformation, both on the continent and in England, was much more radical in its attitude to liturgy. This was not just a negative reaction against the formalism and unreality of so much contemporary ecclesiastical worship. Nor was it, in this country, a mere rebound from the attempted imposition of the Book of Common Prayer. It was rather the outcome of an intensely positive conviction, derived from scripture, that all true worship is a response to the presence and activity of the Holy Spirit in the hearts of the assembled worshippers. It was essentially a resurgence of the spontaneous and free, the charismatic and prophetic worship of the primitive church. The Anabaptists, the extreme Separatists, and the Quakers rejected all liturgical forms as a 'stinting' or quenching of the Holy Spirit. In the interests of 'inspired spontaneity' all 'stilted forms' were jettisoned. Deep suspicion was felt towards the premeditated in any form, to either prayer or preaching prepared before the service. Exposition of scripture and preaching were extempore, or at least the use of a manuscript was frowned upon. The spiritual worship issuing from the heart had no love of or need for words read from a book. In some assemblies even the reading of passages from scripture, or preaching from an open Bible was suspect. Read prayers, and psalms or hymns sung together from a book, were alike proscribed. In practice this freedom was usually controlled by the knowledge and use of the scriptures and by the administration of the gospel ordinances. The

[1] R. Abba, *Principles of Christian Worship*, 108.

Quakers, however, rejected the sacraments and subordinated scripture to the inner light, to the immediate revelations of the Holy Spirit. At this extreme, liturgy has been rejected and liberty enthroned.

10. The nature and purpose of liturgy

From this survey of the relationship and tension between freedom and order, liberty and liturgy in scripture and church history, we pass on to a consideration of the place and function of both in our worship today. We begin with liturgy, which can only be rightly evaluated if its true nature is understood. A good deal of confusion results from the fact that the connotation of the phrase 'the liturgy' tends to differ according to the ecclesiastical tradition of those employing it. In the Eastern Orthodox churches the phrase is commonly used as a description of the eucharistic rite. In the west, it is widely used to describe all the written, fixed, and prescribed services of the church. Both these usages have given rise to the misleading but widespread assumption that a liturgy is *necessarily* a form or type of service, all the words of which are written down, prescribed by authority and constantly repeated. This is to define liturgy in terms of one particular manifestation of it, a contraction of meaning analogous to defining 'agape' in terms of 'charity'. That liturgy can, and for long periods has taken a fixed, prescribed, and written form is true; that it has always and must of necessity take that form is false. In the New Testament *leitourgia* is the service rendered by man to God, or (which is another way of saying the same thing) by man to man. The word is used, for example, of the priestly service of Zechariah in the temple, and of the practical service of the Corinthians in contributing money for the relief of needy Christians at Jerusalem.[1] Liturgy is the work of the People of God, whether assembled or dispersed; that is to say, it is both worship and service. Although the two are inseparable, we are here concerned with the former aspect.

When the people of God are assembled, the liturgy 'is the place of redemptive encounter between the church and her ascended Lord, the vehicle of divine action and human response. To this end it must, in pattern and structure, be theologically rooted, biblically based'.[2] It is the continuing responsibility of the church to ensure that the pattern

---

[1] Luke 1. 23; 2 Cor. 9. 12.   [2] N. Clark, *Call to Worship*, 12.

and structure is such that *the whole gospel* is declared and expressed. The liturgy must also be an adequate vehicle for the reverse movement, the response, enabling the congregation, in union with all the saints militant and triumphant, to offer full and acceptable worship to God. That is to say, as a pattern or structure, the liturgy is the servant of the dialogue, the vehicle of divine revelation and human response. This revelation, given in the history of Israel, and in the ministry, death, and resurrection of Jesus Christ, the living and incarnate Word, is 'traditioned' in worship. The liturgy is the servant of tradition (*paradosis*). It is the means whereby that which has been received from the Lord is delivered to us. The function of liturgy is to transmit and make contemporary the prophetic and apostolic tradition enshrined in the scriptures, together with the living tradition of the People of God down the ages, 'the garnered excellence of the saints'. It is the vehicle which brings the past into the present. The liturgy is also the servant of the fellowship (*koinonia*) as well as of the tradition. It enables the people to respond *together* to the revelation of God. For if Christians are to worship corporately, there must be a customary or agreed procedure, a pattern of word and action, however simple and rudimentary. A good liturgy is a servant of the gospel and the church, a means and not an end. Here the saving deeds of God in Christ are 'traditioned' and the adoring response of the people is offered. The former activity takes place through the reading of the scriptures, the preaching of the word, the celebration of the sacraments and the observance of the Christian year. If, on the other hand, there is to be a full corporate response, some provision must be made for common praise and prayer. The liturgy exists to make possible this reciprocal activity of proclamation and adoration. Thus understood, liturgy is not the foe but the friend of liberty.

11. Worship by the Spirit

'Where the Spirit of the Lord is, there is liberty.'[1] This pregnant utterance has two implications for our worship of far reaching importance. The Holy Spirit is the Spirit of the Lord, of the risen and glorified Lord Jesus Christ, who is the same today as yesterday. Of the Paraclete, Jesus said, 'He will take what is mine and declare it to you.'[2] The Spirit interprets, transmits, and contemporizes the revelation and redemption

[1] 2 Cor. 3. 17. N.E.B.   [2] John 16. 15.

made once for all; by his inspiration and activity Jesus Christ is 'traditioned' in the church. The Spirit operates through that which is handed
down; the apostolic *paradosis* is the means of truth and grace. That is
why, in so far as liturgy transmits and declares the full historic gospel,
it is a channel of the Holy Spirit in the church. It was this aspect of
truth that Puritans, Separatists, and Quakers tended to overlook or
deny. In justifiable reaction against contemporary ecclesiastical tradition and worship, and failing to distinguish between things that differ,
they rejected the good with the bad, and threw ecclesiastical tradition
and liturgy out of the ark of salvation. 'It must be agreed that the
puritan criticism of Catholic liturgy, that it is so constructed as to
prevent the Holy Spirit breaking through at any point, is grossly
unfair. That criticism suffers itself from too rigid a conception of the
Holy Spirit's working, one which assumes that the Spirit works only
on the conscious level and in the allegedly spontaneous fashion expressed
by "conceived" as opposed to "set" prayer.'[1]

On the other hand, the true glory, the positive achievement of the
Puritans, the Separatists, and their successors lay in their rediscovery
and reaffirmation of the truth – 'where the Spirit of the Lord is, there
is liberty'. They had a lively apprehension of the fact that vital worship
depends upon the presence and activity of the Holy Spirit. Apart from
him, we may 'tune our formal songs', but there will be no praise; we
may say prayers, but there will be no prayer. They saw clearly that
patterns and forms, rites and ceremonies, may be 'faultily faultless,
icily regular, splendidly null'.[2] They knew from experience that
formalism, the use of forms apart from the inspiration of the Spirit,
was a deadly enemy to true worship. They sought therefore to make
room, ample room, in the assembly for the movement, the inspiration, the spontaneity of the Holy Spirit. Their historic protest against
the inflexible, rigid, stylized liturgies of Roman Catholicism and
Anglicanism is in full accord with the worship of the primitive
church.

This legacy of freedom in worship is of abiding value and significance. For Jesus Christ is the Lord and king of scripture and tradition,
and the liturgy is the servant, not the master. The Jesus Christ of today
is present within the assembly, and his Spirit may give new guidance
and elicit a fresh response. He is the Master, not the liturgical pattern,

---

[1] D. Jenkins, *Tradition and the Spirit*, 188.   [2] Tennyson, *Maud*.

and we must not dethrone him by making that which is secondary, primary. 'Liturgical expression which is equated with sacramental life puts bonds upon the kingly freedom of the ascended Lord, domesticates the untamed movements of the Spirit, and confines the inner life of the people of God to the trappings of its historical and cultural past.'[1] The church which understands the true nature and purpose of the liturgy will safeguard the liberty of God's people, strive for flexibility rather than rigidity, and be prepared from time to time to reform her worship under the guidance of the word and the Spirit. Two things are essential if Christians are to 'worship by the Spirit of God', liberty in preaching and liberty in prayer. While loyal to scripture, and rooted in the tradition of the church, the minister of the word must be free to say with Micaiah, 'As the Lord lives, what the Lord says to me, that I will speak.'[2] Furthermore, as was stressed above, the nature of Christian worship is determined by the fact that 'God has sent the Spirit of his Son into our hearts, crying "Abba! Father!"' As sons of God, in the intimacy of trust and love, Christians must be free to speak to God, whether in private or in the assembly, as the Spirit moves and directs. Such prayer may be prepared before the service (free prayer) or offered spontaneously during the service (extempore prayer). For the Spirit works through disciplined preparation and through 'inspired spontaneity'. Liturgies which provide ample room for free proclamation and free prayer are in harmony with the basic principles of scripture and with the practice of the primitive church.

12. Common order

If liberty and liturgy are alike essential to the fulness of Christian worship, how then are they to be combined? In making this combination we should seek to avoid two dangers, the extremes found in church history. At the one extreme is the prescribed, inflexible, excessively stylized liturgy which leaves little or no room for variation and adaptation, for the spontaneity and freedom of the Holy Spirit. At the other extreme is the disorder and anarchy, the subjectivism and individualism, the 'squalid sluttery' and poverty of content which results when the traditional pattern and forms of Christian worship are jettisoned. There are two main ways of combining liberty and

[1] N. Clark in *The Pattern of the Church*, ed. by A. Gilmore, 162.
[2] I Kings 22. 14.

liturgy. The first is the way of *Common Order* and the second is the way of *Common Prayer*. In the former, orders, rubrics, and words for the various services of the church are provided for guidance, but are not prescribed by ecclesiastical authority. In the latter, they are both provided and prescribed. As indicated in this chapter, worship in the temple, in the synagogue, and in the primitive church was, for the most part, based upon the acceptance, tacit or statutory, of common order. As regards order and acts, there was a recognized procedure, customary or enacted. There were rubrics rather than rites. Words were indeed provided, psalms, hymns, confessions, liturgical praises and prayers. Sometimes they were prescribed; more often not. For *Common Order* may approximate in varying degrees to *Common Prayer*. There are two great advantages in refusing to prescribe, as distinct from provide, the words to be used in the various services of the church; spontaneity and relevance. The minister, offering the prayers on behalf of the congregation, is at liberty to respond, in the context of worship itself, to the promptings of the Holy Spirit. Furthermore, he is free to relate and adapt the prayers to the aspirations, needs, and circumstances of the worshippers. 'For it is not possible that forms of prayer should be composed, that are perfectly suited to all our occasions in the things of this life and the life to come. Our circumstances are always altering in this frail and mutable state.'[1] Relevance is the chief merit of 'free prayer' – 'done by some work of meditation *before* we begin to speak in prayer' – which is distinguished by Isaac Watts from 'extempore prayer' – 'when we without any reflection or meditation beforehand address ourselves to God and speak the thoughts of our hearts as fast as we conceive them'. When the prayers are prepared in advance for one particular occasion they can be fitting, appropriate, relevant. This preparation in advance, however, is not *always* necessary, at least for all the prayers, for some ministers have a special gift for extempore prayer. On behalf of the congregation they can speak to God 'as a man speaks to his friend'.[2] We do not usually prepare in advance the words of a conversation with a human friend, still less do we address him with prescribed words. Extempore prayer, warm, direct, intimate, corresponds to the essential nature of prayer as conversation with God. Not all ministers, however, possess this gift of the Spirit. What widespread harm has been and still is being done, by the assumption that

---

[1] Isaac Watts, *Guide to Prayer*, Works 4, 127.   [2] Exod. 33. 11.

what is true of the few is true of all! As Calvin realistically recognized, *Common Order* is necessary, just because there are so many unenlightened and ungifted ministers. If a denomination or communion provides *Common Order*, then the study of liturgy should have absolute priority in the training of the ministry. Only those churches which have a fixed, written liturgy can afford to ignore the teaching of liturgy. 'It is one of the tragedies of the situation that the churches which have given their ministers the maximum liberty of liturgical improvisations are those which have given them the minimum training in liturgical principles.'[1]

13. Common prayer

The phrase *Common Prayer* is used here as a description of those liturgies in which not only the order and rubrics, but also the words to be used in the various services, including the seasonal variations, are written down and prescribed by ecclesiastical authority. Liturgy of this kind has certain weighty advantages. Prepared by gifted men within the worshipping church, and tested and re-shaped over long periods of time, the traditional forms of liturgy are thoroughly scriptural in language and spirit. They enshrine what Dr Percy Dearmer called 'the accumulated wisdom and beauty of the Christian church, the garnered excellence of the saints'. Used alike by Christians in past ages and by contemporary Christians throughout the world, they ensure catholicity of spirit and outlook. The worshippers are delivered from the defects and moods of the minister, and from the imposition of a particular type of piety (however excellent in itself) upon the local church. Order, dignity, and beauty are ensured. Furthermore, a good liturgy has an impressive as well as an expressive function to perform. Because we are frail, imperfect, and sinful we may, on a given occasion, have little to express or offer to God. Liturgy both teaches and inspires us to pray. It quickens the spirit of devotion. On the other hand, if the defects of a set liturgy are to be avoided, if there is to be variation, flexibility, and freedom, certain provisions need to be made within *Common Prayer*. The service book must be liberally provided with 'propers', with prayers which vary according to the season. The rubrics should provide for the use, in most services, of 'occasional prayers to be said at the discretion of the minister', whether provided in the book itself or in other duly

[1] L. Newbigin, *A South India Diary*, 86.

authorized collections. The inclusion of the following rubric in the 1928 Book of Common Prayer, was a move in the right direction. 'Note, that subject to any direction which the Bishop may give, the minister may, at his discretion, after the conclusion of Morning or Evening Prayer, or any Service contained in this Book, offer prayer in his own words.' This, however, is too cautious, does not go nearly far enough. Extempore or free prayer is an essential part of Christian worship and should not be made subject 'to any direction', or relegated to a position 'after the conclusion' of the liturgy. The Book of Common Worship of the Church of South India[1] has taken 'the big leap forward' in the combination of liberty and liturgy. Three times within *An Order for the Lord's Supper* the presbyter has liberty to use other written forms, or to offer prayer in his own words. The second of the three *Orders for Morning and Evening Worship* contains the rubric 'Then follow occasional prayers and thanksgivings, liturgical or extempore.' In the third of these orders, the presbyter is at liberty to use other forms or to offer extempore prayer, no less than five times within the service. Finally, why should all the 'proper prefaces' and other variable prayers themselves be prescribed, as distinct from provided? Why not, as in the primitive church, leave the celebrant free to extemporize at this point? Too risky? Is not boldness rather than caution the mark of the truly apostolic? Such provisions would go far to overcome the defects of fixed liturgy, and make room for the freedom and spontaneity of the Holy Spirit.

14. Both liberty and liturgy

The creation of false antitheses is one of the chief pastimes of the devil. Great harm has been done in the church, especially since the Reformation, by the sterile antithesis between liturgical and free worship. We need both, for both alike are present in scripture and in the primitive church, and neither is made perfect apart from the other. It is a tragic mistake to set freedom and tradition, spontaneity and order in opposition. True freedom is the fruit of discipline, and creative spontaneity is the result of adequate rootage in scripture and tradition. 'It was after Jesus had taken the decisive step of total identification to the utmost with *the traditional pattern* of the lives of his sinful people and after he had gone down into the waters of John's baptism that he

[1] Oxford University Press, 1963.

received the Holy Spirit on the other and yonder side of all human convention and custom and tradition . . . here is the creative *springing out of the traditional*.'[1] As in life, so in worship, the freedom of the Spirit is on the yonder side of tradition. Our response to God 'cannot achieve its full and balanced reality and beauty, unless both order and spontaneity, liturgy and liberty, the ministry of the Word and the ministry of the Sacraments, the work of the prophet and the work of the priest, give it of their best'.[2] Joined together by God, liberty and liturgy should not by man be put asunder.

[1] J. E. Fison, *The Blessing of the Holy Spirit*, 213. Italics mine.
[2] E. Underhill, *Worship*, 91.

Chapter VI

CONGREGATIONAL PARTICIPATION

1. United worship

'MAY the God of steadfastness and encouragement grant you to live in such harmony with one another, in accord with Christ Jesus, that *together* you may *with one voice* glorify the God and Father of our Lord Jesus Christ.'[1] Paul prays for unity in the church, because that will result in unity, harmony, and unanimity in worship. Calvin's comment is, 'The unity of his servants is so much esteemed by God, that he will not have his glory sounded forth amidst discords and contentions.' But if they are living *kata Christon*, in accordance with the character and example of Christ, then all the members of the church will worship God together. It is not here suggested that the phrase 'with one voice' implies that the Christians in Rome at this time repeated out loud together words of praise and prayer, that they had a common written liturgy, although in view of the worship of the synagogue and of the type of worship described in the Apocalypse, the joint repetition of *memorized* formulas, confessions, doxologies etc. cannot be ruled out.[2] But it *is* implied that corporate life will result in corporate worship. There will be a concerted movement of the Holy Spirit in the assembly. All the members of the Body will be actively involved and engaged in the worship of God. Like the various instruments in a great orchestra, they will unite to give glory to God.

In this chapter we are concerned with one important question. To what extent, and in what various ways, should the laity participate in the worship of the church? Christian worship is essentially corporate, communal, congregational. Yet this ideal is very far from realization in many church services today. Whether consciously or unconsciously, whether readily or with reluctance, whether by choice or by tradition, the ordained ministry has usurped many of the functions of the laity in worship. This is not the place to discuss the doctrine of the church or of the ministry. It is here assumed that the whole church is the priestly

[1] Rom. 15. 5, 6. [2] Cf. Acts 4. 24.

Body of Christ in the world, *and* that by his intention and appointment, there is also a special ministry within and to the church. These two affirmations we regard not as contradictory, but as complementary. The acceptance of the ordained ministry as appointed by Christ should not, however, blind us to the evils of clericalism and sacerdotalism. And the usurpation by clergy and ministers of many of the functions of the laity, especially in the sphere of worship, has resulted in what is perhaps the greatest weakness of the church today, the passivity of the laity. 'Participation is the secret of interest.' In the sphere of education this principle is well known and widely accepted. That church worship is, in the minds of many, associated with dullness, is due in no small measure to the exclusion of the people from active participation in it. If we are to overcome 'our deadly and ever-present enemy, boredom',[1] we must encourage congregational participation. We shall look first at worship in the Bible and in the history of the church, in order to study, at widely separated periods, the parts taken respectively by the special ministry and by the laity within it. Having done this, we shall then consider in what various ways congregations today can be encouraged and helped to take a more active part in the worship of the church.

2. Two Old Testament examples

Two examples of lay activity may be given from ancient Hebrew worship. In the ceremony of the presentation of the first-fruits,[2] the Deuteronomic author quotes (in verses 5b to 10a) and preserves an ancient confession which probably antedates the erection of Solomon's temple. At harvest time, the Israelite was required to put the first-fruits of his produce into a basket, and to take it to the central sanctuary. There the gift was to be handed over to the priest; or, according to the earlier account, he himself was to set it down before the altar. This action was accompanied and interpreted by a declaration of faith, which began with the words, 'A wandering Aramean was my father.' This confession, recited by the layman himself, commemorated the mighty acts of God, the exodus and the conquest of Canaan. To the grace of God thus revealed in his saving deeds in history, the worshipper responded with gratitude, expressed in gift and confession, in prostration and rejoicing. In this combination 'of prophetic interpretation and

---

[1] G. Michonneau, *Revolution in a City Parish*, 28.   [2] Deut. 26. 1–11.

priestly ritual',[1] *the layman was active throughout,* both in what was said
and in what was done.

   This was true also of the ancient 'peace-offering'. In primitive times,
before the centralization of worship at Jerusalem, the Israelite and his
family, or the headmen and people of a city, would drive an animal
to the place of sacrifice, usually a high-place just outside the city. After
laying on his hands to identify himself with it, the layman himself
killed the victim. The blood and certain parts of the sacrifice were
offered to God. The offering was usually accompanied by words, of
penitence, gratitude, or petition, or by song and dance. The sacrifice
was consummated in communion, the communal meal, which took
place either in the open air or in 'the hall' adjacent to the high-place.[2]
By feasting on the flesh of the victim, part of which had already been
offered by fire to God, the worshippers had fellowship with God and
with one another. What part had the priests in all this? The answer
will depend upon place and period. Originally, anyone could offer
sacrifice, the head of the family or clan, the headsmen of the village or
town, the king as leader of the people.[3] On the other hand, from time
immemorial, the local sanctuaries had their priests. Theirs was a dual
task, to give oracles, and to supervise the offerings according to the
tradition of the high-place. Leviticus describes the respective parts of
priest and layman in the peace-offerings at the central sanctuary.[4] Even
at this later stage, *the layman does far more than the priest.* The latter
dashes the blood against the altar, and burns upon it the portions
offered to God, but the layman participates in the activity at every
stage. He it was who selected the unblemished gift (one of his own
domestic animals), took it to the sanctuary, and identified himself with
it by the laying on of hands. He it was who killed the victim and,
either directly, or indirectly through the priest, offered the blood and
the portions to God. He himself offered praise and prayer and presided
at the communal meal, the joyful feast in which all the worshippers
participated. If the priest was there at all, he was there to do it with,
not for, the layman.

3. Temple worship

With the growth of sacerdotalism in Israel, the participation of
laymen in the cult decreased. In primitive times, the layman served as

---

[1] H. Wheeler Robinson, *Inspiration and Revelation in the Old Testament,* 215.
[2] 1 Sam. 9. 22.   [3] 1 Sam. 20. 29; 9. 12. 2 Sam. 6. 17.   [4] Lev. 3. 1–17.

priest, and sacrifice was offered by patriarch and king, by the head of the family or of the community. No special order of priests was required for the celebration of the cult. Yet, at the same time, the priests *were* also there, giving oracles and supervising the offerings, at the high-places and the sanctuaries. It was possible for the priest to supervise without superseding the activity of the layman in offering sacrifice. As described above, the activity in the personal or domestic sacrifice was predominantly that of the layman, within which the priest had some part. But with the centralization of worship at Jerusalem, and the elaboration of the cult, the activity of the layman in worship was, to a large extent, taken over by the priest. True, in the offering of a personal or domestic sacrifice at the central sanctuary, the Israelite still had some part. Yet in the case of a communal or national sacrifice, he had virtually no part. Like a worshipper at a medieval Mass, he was now the spectator of an elaborate ritual, performed by the priestly caste.

This change of emphasis from a predominantly lay to a predominantly priestly worship, can be seen in that full and beautiful description of the temple service which we owe to Ben Sira.[1] This late passage, belonging to the second century B.C., must not of course be read as a description of the kind of worship offered at Solomon's temple before the exile. This same tendency, however, to hand over worship to the priestly-expert must have been present at the central sanctuary from the beginning. Increasing emphasis on the holiness and transcendence of God intensified the process. Ben Sira begins by describing the splendour of the High Priest Simon, as he comes forth from 'the house of the veil' on the day of Atonement. Standing at the altar, surrounded by 'all the sons of Aaron in their splendour', he arranges the rows of wood for kindling the burnt offering, and takes the sacrificial portions from the hands of the priests. Having kindled the offering, he then pours out 'a libation of the blood of the grape' at the foot of the altar, 'a pleasing odour to the Most High, the King of all'. The participation of three distinct orders or groups of people in the sacrificial worship is then described. 'Then the sons of Aaron shouted, they sounded the trumpets of hammered work, they made a great noise to be heard for remembrance before the Most High. Then all the people together made haste and fell to the ground upon their faces to worship their Lord, their Almighty, God Most High. And the singers praised him with their

---

[1] Eccles. 50. 1–21.

voices in sweet and full-toned melody. And the people besought the
Lord Most High in prayer before him who is merciful, till the order of
the worship of the Lord was ended; so they completed his service.
Then Simon came down, and lifted up his hands over the whole
congregation of the sons of Israel, to pronounce the blessing of the
Lord with his lips, and to glory in his name; and they bowed down in
worship a second time, to receive the blessing from the Most High.'

Here is a service, spectacular and colourful, performed by profes-
sionals on behalf of the people, whose participation is severely limited.
The layman is no longer involved in the direct action of selecting,
bringing, giving, slaying, and offering the victim. All this is done by
the high priest and 'the sons of Aaron'. There is also a professional
choir; the Levites chant the psalms to instrumental accompaniment.[1]
What is left to the people? The prostration of their bodies in worship,
and the offering of their personal prayers. It is a liturgy in which each
order has its due part, but the predominant activity is that of the
Aaronic priesthood. Centralization and elaboration are always inimical
to lay participation.

4. Pentecostal worship

In the primitive church there was no distinction, still less contrast,
between priest and layman. *All* those who come to Christ the living
stone, are to be built as living stones into a spiritual temple, for the
holy work of priesthood.[2] The royal priesthood is God's own people,
appointed to offer spiritual sacrifices and to advertise the saving deeds
of the Lord.[3] In this dual task of worship and witness all the members
of the church are to participate. To what extent did the people participate in the worship of the assembly in the apostolic age? The apostle
Paul describes certain aspects of the worship of one Gentile church in
the middle of the first century.[4] We may not assume that this account
of the worship of the church at Corinth can be applied without qualification to every other local church in the apostolic age. No doubt in a
Jewish Christian congregation, the influence of synagogue worship,
with its prayers, lessons, and exposition would be much more in evidence. Apparently the synagogue tradition had little influence upon
the Corinthian church, with its high valuation of spontaneity and

[1] Cf. Amos 5. 23.   [2] 1 Peter 2. 5. N.E.B. margin.
[3] 1 Peter 2. 5, 9   [4] 1 Cor. 14.

enthusiasm, *glossolalia* and direct revelation. Furthermore, a distinctive ministry of function, still less of office, is not discernible within this young and turbulent Gentile church. We select this chapter not in order to generalize from it, but as an outstanding example of the active participation of the entire community in the service. Here all the members of the church are free to contribute something to the worship under the unfettered movement and inspiration of the Holy Spirit. 'To sum up, my friends: when you meet for worship, *each of you contributes* a hymn, some instruction, a revelation, an ecstatic utterance, or the interpretation of such a utterance.'[1]

This may be an ideal picture. Perhaps *every* member of the assembly did not in fact contribute something to the service. But two facts are beyond dispute. All (certainly all the men) were free to take part, and many were in the habit of doing so. The disorders the apostle seeks to rectify were due precisely to such a widespread and enthusiastic participation. In the verse just quoted, five types of contribution to the service are cited. As in other Pauline lists, these examples are typical rather than exhaustive. Paul is also concerned that those who are listening should also be involved. Prophecy is superior to ecstatic utterance because it builds up the church. This it does because, unlike *glossolalia*, it is addressed to and involves the understanding of all the worshippers. Prayer to God 'in a tongue' is of limited value, because the other members of the assembly cannot understand what is being said. Paul insists that the service as a whole should be in the vernacular, not 'in the tongues of men and of angels', but in a language understood by the people. *Participation is dependent upon intelligibility.* It is because the apostle starts from the conviction that worship should be a social event, a communal experience, that he seeks not to abolish, but to regulate, speaking with tongues.

I Corinthians 14 illustrates the dangers of pentecostal worship; blatant egoism, the desire to show off, rivalry, the over-valuation of the spectacular, emotionalism, individualism, the negative reaction of the outsider, disorder. It is significant, however, that in setting out to inculcate due order, the apostle does not suppress this type of worship. He makes no attempt to enforce a prescribed order or sequence, or to confine participation to a special ministry or order within the community. In ensuring that 'all things should be done decently and in

[1] I Cor. 14. 26. N.E.B.

H

order',[1] he does not limit congregational participation or quench the Holy Spirit. This ideal of full community participation has continued to haunt the church. Its influence can be seen in the Montanists of the second and the Quakers of the seventeenth century. In more recent times, the (Plymouth) Brethren and the Pentecostals have sought to recover this type of worship.

5. Ante-Nicene worship

The whole Body is a royal priesthood; yet within it there are varieties of gift. Not all its members participate to the same degree or in the same way in the service of God. The description of worship at Corinth must be supplemented by the knowledge that in the church as a whole, from the beginning, there was a special ministry of function and of office. This special ministry did not exclude the active and widespread participation of gifted men in church worship and service. Yet from the beginning, the apostles, the prophets, and the elders or overseers had special functions in the church and in the churches. New circumstances and needs resulted in the establishment and development of other ministries; deacons, messengers, teachers, bishops,[2] apostolic delegates. The emergence and growth of these various ministries did not mean that the worship of the assembly was 'conducted' by any one man or monopolized by any one group. 'In the early church the deliberate effort was made to divide up the functions of worship among as many people as possible.'[3] Speaking of the ante-Nicene period as a whole, the corporate character of Christian worship was still largely maintained. Presiding at the eucharist, the bishop, *the* pastor of the local church, preached the word and offered the great eucharistic prayer. He was surrounded and assisted by the presbyters, who in course of time acted as his representatives in other local churches. The deacons, too, had their place in the liturgy, in the intercessions, in leading the responses of the people, in the reading of the scriptures, in the distribution of the elements at the communion. The people themselves brought the bread and wine and a variety of other gifts, and presented them at the offertory. They exchanged the kiss of peace, shared in the praise, responded to the prayers, and

[1] 1 Cor. 14. 40.
[2] The elders, of course, were bishops. Here the reference is to the emergence of *the* presiding elder.
[3] A. G. Hebert, *Liturgy and Society*, 75.

received the consecrated bread and wine. Each group had a recognized part within the common worship, the liturgy of the people of God.

6. 'The great disaster'

It was a gradual and uneven process by which the people were excluded or by negligence fell away from active participation in church worship. There is not just one, but a number of reasons. The move from house to basilica, the transformation of domestic into public worship, were factors militating against the active participation of the people. What was once possible in a small, closely-knit fellowship, became difficult, if not impossible, in a large congregation which was no longer a community. Corporate worship presupposes the existence of *koinonia;* this was to a large extent lost as the 'brotherhood throughout the world'[1] was transformed into a hierarchical institution. For, in the course of time, the special ministry of function and office became a professional class, a sacerdotal order within the church. The clergy were set over against the laity, and the worship of the church became the special domain of the priestly hierarchy. 'The theology of fear' contributed to this process. The eucharist became a dread mystery. The people were afraid to approach the holy table, or to communicate, lest they should suffer the fate of Uzzah when he took hold of the Ark of God. The development of ceremonial and the elaboration of the rite also had the effect of excluding the people. Simplicity and congregational involvement go hand in hand; to elaborate worship is to hand it over to the expert. Added momentum was given to these incipient tendencies and developments by the state recognition of the church, and the rapid inclusion of large numbers of nominal Christians within it. The ultimate outcome was 'the great disaster',[2] the celebration of the eucharist by the priest without lay communicants. The people became spectators of a rite, mysterious, elaborate, and inaudible, in which they had little or no part. When Latin was no longer understood by the common people, even when audible the rite was unintelligible. The Mass came to be regarded as the action of the priest at the altar; the loss of congregational participation was almost complete.

[1] I Peter 5. 9.
[2] Y. Brilioth, *Eucharistic Faith and Practice*, 279.

H[2]

7. The legacy of the Reformation

Did the Reformation give back to the people their rightful place in church worship? Some great gains were made in this direction. There was a new understanding of the church, a recovered awareness of the congregation of the Lord, assembled to hear and obey his word. Latin was abolished and the vernacular introduced; the common people understood once more what was being said or read in the church service. In the reading of the scriptures, the offering of the prayers, and the preaching of the word, the mind and understanding were engaged and occupied. Intelligibility is the friend of participation. No less important, the praises of God were put back into the mouths of the people, although this did not happen everywhere or immediately. Formerly, psalms and hymns had been sung by monks, by clergy, or experts 'in choir'. They now became congregational acts of praise. Luther composed hymns and Calvin, following the Strasbourg reformers, encouraged the singing of metrical psalms. With the advent in the eighteenth century of Isaac Watts and Charles Wesley, congregational praise was greatly enriched, and achieved the important role it now has in Protestant churches throughout the world. In some of the reformation liturgies the vocal participation of the laity in the common prayers was also made possible. The Book of Common Prayer is a fine example of this. In Morning and in Evening Prayer, the congregation says or sings 'with one voice' the general confession, the psalms, the canticles, the creed, and the various responses.

These great gains were, however, offset by serious failures. These were partly due to the fact that the reformers were inescapably men of their own generation, inheritors of the individualism and clericalism of the medieval church. Three serious weaknesses in the reformation legacy may here be noted. The first is the survival of clericalism, evident in the continued ministerial domination of the service. Worship remained what it had been before the Reformation, largely the concern and prerogative of one man. In this realm, as in others, 'new presbyter' was 'but old priest writ large'.[1] The baneful influence of Zwingli who, at Zürich, excluded singing, banished common prayer, reduced the congregation to silence, and turned the whole of the Sunday 'preaching service' into a ministerial monologue, has been

[1] J. Milton, 'On the New Forcers of Conscience under the Long Parliament'.

widespread. To this day in protestantism, especially in the Reformed, the Puritan and Free Church traditions church worship is dominated by the man in the pulpit to whom most of the service has been, readily no doubt, handed over. He reads the scriptures, offers the prayers, preaches the word, and administers the sacraments with a minimum of assistance. Apart from singing, the congregation is reduced to the role of listening. This one aspect, itself important and essential, has been made almost the whole. In the average Free Church service the people sit listening to the voice of one man for about three-quarters of the whole period of worship.

This ministerial domination of worship is closely bound up with a second weakness. The error of verbalism is the assumption that worship is largely, if not entirely, a matter of words. In stressing the paramount importance of the word of God, read and preached, and reacting violently against the Mass and elaborate ceremonialism of the medieval church, some of the reformers and their successors swung to the opposite extreme. Ritual was regarded with profound suspicion, reduced to a bare minimum, or excluded from worship altogether. Verbalism militates against congregational involvement, for the ordinary worshipper, without the gift of eloquence, finds it easier to do something rather than to say something.

A third serious weakness is the failure of *some* traditions to make provision for vocal participation in common prayer. True, in the immediate post-Reformation era, the reformed (i.e. Calvinistic) churches had common order and liturgical prayer. But the text was in the hands of the minister only. The people had no prayer book, and vocal participation in any of the prayers (other than the Lord's Prayer) was impossible. It is also true that 'the Puritan tradition in which Baptists, Congregationalists, and Presbyterians stand does not, when considered as a whole, commit its heirs to any one particular form of prayer. Within Puritanism itself we find a variety of liturgical emphases, ranging from a radical repudiation of set forms, including the Lord's Prayer, to the attempt in 1584 to substitute "a Booke of the Form of Common Prayers" for the Anglican Prayer Book as the uniform liturgy of the land'.[1] But in fact most of the heirs of the Puritans did commit themselves to one way of praying. Extempore or unpremeditated prayer has an important place in Christian worship. But if no

[1] R. Abba, *Principles of Christian Worship*, 108.

other way of praying is permitted or practised, then a congregation is deprived of all the complementary advantages of liturgical prayer. Outstanding among these is vocal congregational participation. These three serious weaknesses (ministerial domination of the service, verbalism, and the lack of provision for vocal participation in prayer) must be overcome, if there is to be within the Reformed and Free Church traditions a full restoration of congregational participation. One of the aims of the liturgical movement, perhaps its chief objective, 'is the restoration of the active participation by the people in the official worship of the Church'.[1] According to the weaknesses, deficiencies, or distortions to be overcome, this must necessarily assume different forms within the various traditions and communions. Let us now consider various ways in which this objective, the active participation of the people in worship, can be encouraged and achieved today.

8. Architecture and action

We begin with certain externals which, while not of primary importance, are by no means unimportant. Architecture, especially interior design, can be a hindrance or a help to congregational involvement. A building can be so badly designed as to make corporate worship difficult, and in some cases well-nigh impossible. A church should not be a large auditorium with lofty pupit and galleries. A long-vista building, with lengthy nave, with a chancel behind a screen, and with the Lord's table at the far end, is also inimical to corporate worship. God is not 'out there' at the east end of the church; he is present in the church, the assembly of his people. The building should not have transepts, or any kind of seating arrangement that separates one group of worshippers from another. Rather, it should be designed in such a way that the family of God can be seated round his table, as one. The Lord's table itself should be in such a position that the minister and his assistants can sit behind it, and the people be arranged on the other three sides. Whether the church is round or octagonal, square or rectangular, the interior should be so arranged as to keep the whole congregation together, and in sight of one another and the central action. Elliptical and terraced seating can be a great aid to congregational participation. The sanctuary proper, where the action takes place, should be spacious

[1] 'Liturgical Movement', in *The Oxford Dictionary of the Christian Church*, ed. by F. L. Cross.

and easy of access; it should not be separated from the people by a barrier of any kind. The provision of a lectern as well as a pulpit, of a prayer-desk as well as the pastor's chair behind the table (from which the service should be conducted), will facilitate the participation of trained laymen in the readings and in the prayers.

The building should be designed not only for speaking and listening, but also for movement and action. While acknowledging the primary importance of the word of God, we must avoid the error of verbalism. God's word is also deed; and we can respond to that word in what we do, as well as in what we say. Since the body can participate in prayer, there should be facilities for kneeling, as well as for standing and sitting. Central and side aisles should be wide enough for processions, especially for the offertory procession at the eucharist, when the representatives of the people bring forward the gifts of bread, wine, and wealth. The ritual acts, the entrance of the Bible, the offering of gifts, baptizing, the laying on of hands, the breaking of the bread, the pouring of the wine, should be so performed that the eyes, as well as the ears, of the people are involved in the worship. In short, a church should be designed not only as a place where we sit and listen, but also as a place where we see, move, and act.[1]

9. 'Understanded of the people'

We turn next to the language used in the church building. If the people are to be fully involved, this must be intelligible to them. As we have seen, the apostle Paul contended for intelligibility in worship. 'If you in a tongue utter speech that is not intelligible, how will anyone know what is said? For you will be speaking into the air . . . in church I would rather speak five words with my mind, in order to instruct others, than ten thousand words in a tongue.'[2] Paul set a high valuation on those elements in worship which engaged the understanding of the hearers. There was Jewish precedent for this attitude. When Hebrew became a dead language, the Targums, the Aramaic paraphrases of the law and the prophets, had enabled the people to understand the scriptures. Before the Reformation, Latin had long been a dead language, understood by only a small minority of educated people. By

---

[1] For the application of the principles of Christian worship to the design of the church building, the reader is referred to the excellent book by Basil Minchin, *Outward and Visible*.

[2] 1 Cor. 14. 9, 19.

abolishing the use of Latin in the services, and introducing the vernacular, the reformers made it possible for the laity to participate more fully
in worship. 'It is plainly repugnant to the Word of God, and the custom of the primitive Church, to have public prayer in the church, or
to minister the Sacraments in a tongue not understanded of the people.'[1]
Is the language we use in our services today understood by the common
people? To what extent are they prevented from understanding what
is being read or said by the use of theological, technical, or archaic
words? Do ministers speak 'the language of Zion' rather than that of
wayfaring men?

It is not implied that everything in the service should be perfectly
clear and obvious. The whole personality, and not just the understanding of man should be involved in the worship of God. 'Known God
is no God.' 'With reverence and awe'[2] we worship the high and lofty
one, whose judgments are unsearchable, whose ways are past finding
out. It is however, reasonable to require that the words specifically
addressed to the understanding should be intelligible to the congregation as a whole. Do our hymns, psalms, lessons, and sermons meet this
test? Is it possible, for example, to justify the chanting of *the whole* of
the Psalter in public worship? For apart from a knowledge of the background, some of the psalms are completely unintelligible.[3] Is it right
to read the Bible in a language over three centuries old? When the
scripture reading is from the prophets or the epistles in the Authorized
Version, is the language 'understanded of the people'? It is not suggested that the problem of communication, especially in preaching, can
be solved merely by the use of simple words or basic English. The more
difficult task is to translate the images and metaphors, the ideas and
thought-forms of the ancient scriptures into the thought and language
of the twentieth century, without losing revealed truth in the process.
There is no easy answer: no one simple answer: and indeed no complete
answer at all. In every generation the church must continue to wrestle
with this intractible problem. On the one hand, Christians must be
assiduously taught the language of the Bible: on the other hand 'he
who speaks' must make a disciplined effort to be understood. Intelligent
participation is encouraged and increased when the language used in

---

[1] Articles of Religion, *Book of Common Prayer*, number 24.
[2] Heb. 12. 28.
[3] What, for example, would the average worshipper make of Psalm 60, in any version?

the service is contemporary not archaic, concrete not abstract, common not technical. Basic English promotes corporate participation. 'I design plain truth for plain people; therefore, of set purpose, I abstain from all nice and philosophical speculations; from all perplexed and intricate reasonings; and, as far as possible, even from the show of learning. I labour to avoid all words which are not easy to be understood, all which are not used in common life; and, in particular, those kinds of technical terms that so frequently occur in Bodies of Divinity; those modes of speaking which men of reading are intimately acquainted with, but which to common people are in unknown tongue.'[1] We do well to follow this intention and example of John Wesley.

10. Everyone contributing

The people who meet in the well-designed building, where worship is offered in an intelligible language, should also be free to take part in the service. The opportunity should be provided, at least on some occasions, for the members of a church to contribute something to the worship. For why should they be restricted to singing and giving? Here we revert for guidance to the pentecostal worship of the church at Corinth. Full participation was seen to be the outstanding characteristic. 'When you meet for worship each of you contributes.' The apostle takes this for granted. 'The really notable thing about an early church service must have been that almost everyone came feeling that he had both the privilege and the obligation of contributing something to it. A man did not come with the sole intention of being a passive listener. He did not come only to receive, he came also to give.'[2] As the fire of enthusiasm and devotion died down, and the professional ministry developed, the church as a whole lost this element of charismatic worship. It was recovered, although not in the same form, by the Society of Friends, and more recently by the Brethren and the Pentecostals. 'The respectable churches' (an expression used by the Pentecostals without, apparently, either humour or malice), afraid of disorder, embarrassed by enthusiasm, suspicious of emotion, have long since become adept at quenching the fire of the Holy Spirit. Two

---

[1] From the introduction to a volume of Wesley's sermons, dated 1746; quoted by W. E. Sangster in *Power in Preaching*, 68.
[2] W. Barclay, *The Letters to the Corinthians*, 150.

widespread assumptions about pentecostal worship should be questioned; that, while characteristic of the infancy of the church, it should have no equivalent in our services today; and that it is necessarily an alternative to the ministry of trained and ordained men. It is helpful to remember that the worship of the assembly described in 1 Corinthians 14 would take place in the guest-room of a house. It was domestic, rather than public, worship. Was the church of God at Corinth just one large assembly in the house of Titius Justus,[1] or were there a number of small house-churches? In all our thinking about worship must we start with the assumption that the unit is a congregation in a church building, the larger the better?

The best way to recover and express the charismatic element in worship is to begin with the small unit, the house-church, the week-night fellowship, the Bible study group, the prayer meeting. In the small, closely-knit fellowship or group, the people should be encouraged and trained to contribute to Bible study, to ask questions, to discuss problems of belief and conduct, to share experience, to give testimony, to lead in prayer. In small churches, the people should be given the opportunity of contributing to the Sunday worship. The prayers, for example, need not always be offered by the minister. There can be an 'open' period for intercession at the service of the word or for thanksgiving at the Lord's Supper. As many people as time permits should be given the opportunity to offer concise vocal prayers. Such freedom may be abused, especially by the person who likes the sound of his own voice. But abuse is not a valid argument against right use. Abuses can be avoided or eliminated by teaching, example, and correction. Caution is not a cardinal Christian virtue, and decorum can become deadly. Neither should be allowed to deprive a church of this essential strand in apostolic worship. It would, of course, be naïve in the extreme to suppose that at the *first* opportunity given a large number of people would take part. Unlike the apostle Paul, the minister today will not be faced with the problem of two or three people trying to participate at the same time! The dumb devil is not so easily cast out. A patient ministry of teaching and encouragement is essential. The smouldering embers must be gently fanned into a flame within the small group, before the large congregation is ignited.

[1] Acts 18. 7.

11. Training and using gifted laymen

'Grace was given to each one of us according to the measure of Christ's gift.'[1] Therefore the whole Body is charismatic, and each member is endowed for worship and service. That is why everyone may be expected and required to contribute something to worship. But there is another and complementary kind of participation, that of specially gifted and trained laymen in the services of the church. For 'in a narrower sense, the word (charismatic) is used especially for the supernatural graces which individual Christians need to perform the special tasks incumbent on them in promoting the spiritual advancement of their fellows'.[2] It is significant that, of the nine 'gifts of the Spirit' listed in 1 Corinthians 12. 8–10, as many as six are *special endowments for participation* in the worship of the assembly. Now, as then, there are within the churches gifted laymen who have been endowed by God to participate in worship. As with the athlete or musician, these gifts are appropriated and developed by training. It is the task of the minister to give this training, or to direct them to others more competent to give it. What part should such laymen have in church worship? Five activities may here be mentioned.

As in the apostolic age, gifted laymen should have some part in the ministry of the word. Some may be selected and appointed to represent and serve the congregation by reading the scriptures. From the lectern, one may read the Old and another the New Testament lesson. At the Lord's Supper, the Old Testament and the epistle may be read by laymen, even if the minister reads the gospel. A layman who has been called to preach should be given opportunities to preach to his own, as well as to other churches. He may possibly know less about the Bible, but his experience in the world enables him to relate the word of God to life, and to contribute something of special value to the building up of the Body of Christ. 'And the singers praised him with their voices.' Gifted laymen can also contribute to the ministry of praise. The primary function of a choir is to help and lead the whole congregation in praising God. Unless it does this, it is the enemy of congregational participation. So often choirs want to sing *to* the people or *for* the people, instead of singing *with* the people to God. But if this

[1] Eph. 4. 7.
[2] 'Charismata', in *The Oxford Dictionary of the Christian Church*, 265.

primary purpose is understood and accepted, a choir can contribute in several ways to corporate worship. By singing the appropriate parts of the liturgy, psalms, hymns, canticles, creed, sanctus, gloria in excelsis, to simple settings, a choir can lead and inspire all the people to praise God. A good solo voice, heard in the introit, in the antiphonal singing of the psalms, in sacred song, in gospel hymn, in the solo parts of the anthem, can uplift all hearts to God. And could we not make more use of gifted instrumentalists? The author of Psalm 150 obviously did not assume that one instrument only could be used in the worship of God.

As in reading, preaching, and singing, so also in praying and offering, gifted laymen can contribute to the common act of worship. The ancient function of the deacon, as leader or director of the intercessions and responses of the people, should be revived. From prayer-desk or lectern he may give 'the bidding' for intercession, following which the people pray, as bidden, in the silence. Then either the deacon or the minister may 'collect' the silent prayers in a concise prayer, the probable origin and right use of the collect. The deacon then announces the second bidding, and so on. Suitable laymen should be selected from time to time to offer all the intercessions or the thanksgivings of the people assembled. Finally, as we saw in the Old Testament, in primitive worship the layman was active in offering. In Christian worship the offertory is *par excellence* the function of the laity. The recitation of the offertory sentences, the collection of the gifts, the presentation and offertory prayer, should all be undertaken by laymen. If, in addition to serving at the communion, gifted laymen take some part in all five activities here mentioned, reading, preaching, singing, praying, offering, considerable advance will have been made towards a truly congregational act of worship.

12. Praying from a book

The participation of the people in worship is greatly enhanced by the use of a prayer book. Churches which use a fixed written liturgy have proved the value of this method of praying together. It is one important way of engaging the whole congregation in the activity of prayer. Each is united to all and all to each, and the local congregation is linked with the church in other places and of other ages, who are using or have used the same liturgy. Objectivity, dignity, beauty, order, catholicity, concerted activity, these are some of the values of common prayer. We are not pleading, however, for the use of a fixed written liturgy, with all its limitations and disadvantages, but for the provision of a prayer book which churches are free to use as desired and required. The hymn book is a good analogy. The corporate praise of the church was immeasurably enriched when Christians were able to sing together from a book. Churches which were prejudiced against this had virtually no common praise. Corporate prayer is also immeasurably enriched when an adequate prayer book is provided for the use of the congregation, and the deep-seated prejudice against praying from it has been overcome. As with the hymnal, a church should be free to use or not to use the orders and prayers contained in such a book. Having a fixed, enacted liturgy, and having no written liturgy at all, are alike limitations of freedom. He who is not free to use is not fully free, and he cannot use what is not provided. Prayer, like praise, becomes more truly free and corporate when the people have a book, and are no longer condemned to listen *always* to a solo voice. Of course, it is even better when prayers and responses, as in the synagogue, are memorized, and a book is not required. But the amount of material which can be committed to memory and repeated together in this way is severely limited. The use of a prayer book does not contradict or exclude, but complements and enriches extempore and free prayer.

A prayer book for use in a 'free church' should contain all the psalter suitable for use in Christian worship, together with a large selection of devotional material from other parts of the Bible and from the great liturgies of the church universal.[1] It would contain several complete orders for the celebration of the eucharist, within which the people would be given their part in *the saying* of the prayers. It would also have several complete orders for the service of the word, both for the morning and the evening of the Lord's day. In addition to such orders for whole services, it would contain a large number of shorter acts of worship, of adoration, thanksgiving, confession, supplication, intercession, dedication, for selection and use within other services as required. It would thus be possible to announce and say together a prayer, as it is now possible to announce and sing together a hymn. A prayer book, of course, must be in the hands of all the people and not just of the minister. Little advance in congregational

---

[1] In the book, *Responsive Praises and Prayers for Minister and Congregation* (Hodder and Stoughton), I have attempted to do this.

I

participation is made, simply by providing excellent manuals for ministers. We do not buy a single copy of the hymnal for use in the pulpit only! A prayer book can be a treasury, filled from the Bible and the church, enriching the worship of God's people today, and enabling them to pray together, and with all the saints.

13. The communion of saints

The goal envisaged throughout this chapter, the full participation of the entire congregation in the worship of God, is never in fact realized here on earth. But if this goal is set clearly, attractively, and persistently before a congregation, it is possible to advance and approximate towards the realization of the ideal. In the worship of the church triumphant, the ideal is realized. Looking into heaven, John of Patmos overhears the myriads of myriads of angels saying with a loud voice, 'Worthy is the Lamb who was slain, to receive power and wealth and wisdom and might and honour and glory and blessing.'[1] To this liturgical act of praise, all the creatures in the universe respond with a doxology, which concludes with the *Amen*.[2] Clothed in the white robes of immortality and carrying the palm branches of victory, the saints triumphant cry out *unanimously*, ascribing salvation to God and to the Lamb. The choirs of heaven respond with a liturgical sevenfold doxology.[3] In heaven, there is full participation in worship; in the perfected fellowship of the saints triumphant they all together, with one voice, glorify the God and Father of our Lord Jesus Christ. The church militant here on earth is one with the church triumphant there in heaven. We must therefore worship together with them.

> 'Let saints below in concert sing
> With those to glory gone;
> For all the servants of our King
> In earth and heaven are one.'[4]

As we thus worship within 'the communion of saints', we shall be encouraged and helped towards the realization of the ideal of full participation which they have already achieved. One with the glorious company of the apostles, the goodly fellowship of the prophets, the noble army of martyrs, we shall ourselves be caught up into the whole-

---

[1] Rev. 5. 12.   [2] Rev. 5. 13, 14.   [3] Rev. 7. 9–12.
[4] Charles Wesley.

hearted and unanimous worship of heaven. Because we have already 'come to Mount Zion and to the city of the living God, the heavenly Jerusalem',[1] all true Christian worship takes place in heaven. As we assemble here on earth there comes to us the ancient invitation and command:

'Lift up your hearts!'

The true response of the redeemed must always be:

'We lift them up *unto the Lord* . . . with angels and archangels, and *with all the company of heaven*, we laud and magnify thy glorious name; evermore praising thee and saying: Holy, holy, holy, Lord God of hosts, heaven and earth are full of thy glory: glory be to thee, O Lord most high.   Amen.'

[1] Heb. 12. 22.

INDEX OF NAMES AND SUBJECTS

INDEX OF AUTHORS

INDEX OF SCRIPTURE REFERENCES

OLD TESTAMENT

APOCRYPHA

NEW TESTAMENT